Digital
Photography

Digital Photography

Peter Bargh

TEACH YOURSELF BOOKS

For UK order queries: please contact Bookpoint Ltd, 130 Milton Park, Abingdon, Oxon
OX14 4SB. Telephone: (44) 01235 400414, Fax: (44) 01235 400454. Lines are open from
9.00–6.00, Monday to Saturday, with a 24 hour message answering service.
Email address: orders@bookpoint.co.uk

For U.S.A. & Canada order queries: please contact NTC/Contemporary Publishing,
4255 West Touhy Avenue, Lincolnwood, Illinois 60646–1975, U.S.A.
Telephone: (847) 679 5500, Fax: (847) 679 2494.

Long renowned as the authoritative source for self-guided learning – with more than
30 million copies sold worldwide – the *Teach Yourself* series includes over 200 titles in
the fields of languages, crafts, hobbies, business and education.

British Library Cataloguing in Publication Data
A catalogue record for this title is available from The British Library.

Library of Congress Catalog Card Number: On file

First published in UK 1994 by Hodder Headline Plc, 338 Euston Road, London, NW1 3BH.
This second edition published 2000.

First published in US 1995 by NTC/Contemporary Publishing, 4255 West Touhy Avenue,
Lincolnwood (Chicago), Illinois 60646–1975 U.S.A.

The 'Teach Yourself' name and logo are registered trade marks of Hodder & Stoughton Ltd.

Typeset by Transet Limited, Coventry, England.
Printed in Great Britain for Hodder & Stoughton Educational, a division of Hodder
Headline Plc, 338 Euston Road, London NW1 3BH by Cox & Wyman Ltd, Reading,
Berkshire.

Impression number   10 9 8 7 6 5 4 3 2
Year   2005 2004 2003 2002 2001

CONTENTS

INTRODUCTION

Digital imaging is arguably the most exciting thing to happen to photography since its creation more than 150 years ago. While the principles remain the same – light hits a receptive surface and converts it into an image – the way it does this has changed beyond belief.

Digital photography offers endless possibilities, combining the flexibility of painting with the ease of capture and realism of film photography. The aim of this book is to introduce you to many of these possibilities.

Our journey begins with a brief introduction to digital photography so you can gain an understanding of what a digital picture is, how it differs from conventional film photography and how you can embrace the technology with ease. I will help you make the right choice of equipment by suggesting the essential features of the computer, scanner, camera, software and printer. With a few simple guidelines you'll be able to buy the right tools for the job with confidence.

The main part of the book is split into three basic sections – input, image manipulation and output. **Input** looks at how you take a digital picture and bring it into the computer. Here you will find out how to scan in images, how to use a digital camera, how to download pictures, how to save them and what services you can expect from your processing lab.

Then we travel to the most exciting section – **image manipulation** or, if you prefer, image editing or image retouching. It's here where the fun begins. I'll take you step by step through a range of techniques from simple retouching to advanced skills; all with an easy-to-follow format. You'll learn how to master simple photographic skills, save pounds recreating traditional filter effects, change the weather and touch up your family holiday snaps. I'll even show you how to realise all those weird and wonderful ideas floating around in your head or, if you don't have weird and wonderful ideas floating around in your head, I'll put some there!

The final section is all about **output**. It's here you'll find out how to print your pictures, catalogue them, store them, share them with friends, family or business colleagues, even turn them into presents.

The most important thing is to take your time to discover this exciting new world. Do so and your pictures, and, indeed, your life, will never be the same.

Happy image making!

Peter Bargh

Me and my computer.

1 | WHAT IS A DIGITAL PICTURE?

We've always been fascinated by light and how it can be used to record an image onto any surface – remember chasing your shadow? Inventors took this playschool activity a stage further and developed the *camera obscura* – a box with a lens that focuses light onto a flat surface. People were also aware that light could affect certain substances and change their colour or appearance, but the problem was capturing this change permanently – a problem solved in 1822 by French inventor, Joseph Nicéphore Niépce. Four years later Niépce produced the first successful photograph using a pewter plate coated in bitumen of Judea. He called the technique *heliography* (sun writing) and the exposure took eight hours – a far cry from today's cameras with a 1/12,000 sec top speeds. We have Sir John Herschel to thank for the name *photography* that derives from the Greek words for light and writing. Photography has had inventors, scientists and artists develop new ways of capturing our precious moments on metal, paper, cellulose and film for over 170 years, and now we can add digital to the list.

The modern world

Digital is the buzzword at the beginning of the third millennium. We live in a world in which we are surrounded by digital appliances. We communicate by digital phone, watch the latest news on digital TV, tell the time digitally, even find our way around using digital navigation, and now we can take and store pictures digitally.

A digital picture can be captured and viewed instantly by a digital camera. The picture is then downloaded to a computer where it can be retouched easily using low cost software. With such programs you can remove faults, add or take away bits, change the colour of things, put frames around photos, make your own calendars, stationery, cards, create wacky collages and produce masterpieces from previously mundane snaps. The pictures can then be organised in digital albums, printed, sent as e-mail attachments to friends and relatives around the world or added to your newly created Web site. Digital photography can be something the whole family can enjoy, from taking pictures to editing, through to printing and sharing. The possibilities are endless for the digital photographer, as you'll find as you travel through the units of this book.

For many of us digital photography is new, but capturing pictures digitally has been possible for over 30 years. The reason it's suddenly becoming very appealing is the cost. Only five years ago we had to tolerate computers that ran at a snail's pace, with small storage capacity and huge costs. Today we have machines ten times faster at a fraction of the cost – and specifications continue to rise as prices tumble. Now is definitely the time to consider the digital arena, but before you rush off to buy the latest kit let's take a look at what a digital picture is.

Pixels and chips

Don't expect to find film in a digital camera. Housed behind the lens on the image plane of a digital camera is a silicon charge-coupled device. It's a bit of a mouthful, but we can use the easier acronym CCD.

We can thank Dr George E. Smith of the Bell Laboratories for the invention of the CCD in 1969. By considering how the human brain converts signals received by our eyes, Dr Smith applied the same principles to the CCD. Like the eye, this solid-state, light sensitive chip also converts light into electric signals and processes these signals as a coloured image. Our eyes use cones contained in the fovea centralis to respond to the red, green and blue light while the CCD uses a matrix of colour filtered picture elements.

This grid or bitmap of picture elements (known as pixels) can be surprisingly large considering the CCD is smaller than a standard 35 mm film frame. It's the pixels that make up the digital picture, which may comprise of millions of these tiny coloured squares.

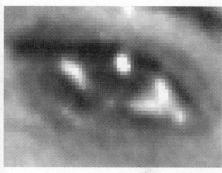

When you enlarge a digital picture you start to see that it's made up of tiny coloured squares, known as pixels. (See colour plate 1.)

Each pixel, although often invisible to the naked eye, has an effect on the overall picture. It's like looking at a woodland scene in summer. On the horizon you see a mass of green. Move closer and the greens can be separated in tone. Closer still and you begin to see the shadow and highlights. Even closer and you see the odd dead brown leaf. Move in and the veins on each leaf become prominent. Grab a magnifying glass and view the subtle changes of tone, textures, insect bites and more. A digital picture is the same. From a distance it's a sharp, well-defined photo, enlarge it and you begin to see that it has jagged edges. Magnify more and the jagged edges become distinct coloured pixels. Keep increasing magnification and you'll end up with an unrecognisable image displayed as a grid of individual colour squares.

Resolution

The quality, or resolution, of a digital picture is partly determined by the number of pixels available. This is established by multiplying the horizontal and vertical values of the useable area of a CCD image sensor. A 640 × 480 pixel CCD, used in basic digital cameras, has a total of 307,200 pixels, while one of the latest super megapixel models employs an 1800 × 1200 array to produce an image with a grand total of 2,160,000 pixels.

Left: The quality you would expect to see when enlarging an image taken with a 640 × 480 pixel camera. Right: The same thing using a 1800 × 1200 pixel camera. (See colour plate 2.)

Both of these pictures will look similar when they're viewed the same size at a distance or at small magnifications, but the pixels will soon become obvious when the lower resolution image is enlarged.

The more pixels you have per inch (ppi) the higher the image resolution, but that does not automatically guarantee sharpness (see Unit 4).

Colour control

The other important consideration is the range of colours achievable from a CCD, technically known as bit depth.

The CCD creates a variable analogue charge, which passes through an analogue-to-digital converter using the black art of binary code – the 0s and 1s stuff you may remember being taught in the dim and distant past in school. Well now's the time to put this knowledge into practice. Digital data are made up of on (0) or off (1) signals – black or white. Each bit of information, which is called a bit, controls the colour of the pixel. A 1-bit image would comprise black or white while a 2-bit image would also include a couple of shades of grey and an 8-bit image has the ability to record 256 shades of grey – just enough for the eye to see a continuous range of tones.

A colour image with continuous tone also has to have 8-bit depth, but for each of the three components – red, green and blue – which gives a potential combined total of 16.7 million colours ($256 \times 256 \times 256$) or a combined 24-bit depth.

Some devices are capable of capturing more colour depth, with up to 16-bits per colour, giving an amazing total of 48-bit colour depth. The chance of spotting whether a CCD has captured this many colours is virtually impossible anyway so we just have to trust the claims of the manufacturers. It's also worth knowing that the billions of colours captured with a 48-bit scanner cannot currently be output, as printers only have 24-bit output. Frustratingly, all the extra data is dumped when you print out the picture. The reassuring thing is that the printer is able to choose which colours to lose, and having a wider choice allows more detail to be captured in the shadow areas.

Digital vs traditional

Benefits of digital

■ You can't accidentally open the back of a digital camera and fog the film.
■ You don't have to buy film.
■ It's easy to catalogue and locate stored pictures.
■ You can view the result as you take it.
■ You can have a hard copy from the camera in minutes.
■ Digital pictures can be manipulated.
■ You can e-mail pictures quickly.

Benefits of film-based camera

■ Quality is better… currently.
■ You don't need a computer.
■ There is a much wider range of features.
■ You have more control with SLR cameras.
■ There is a wider range of accessories.
■ Cameras don't drain batteries quickly.

2 | WHAT YOU NEED TO GET STARTED

If you've just decided to have a go at digital photography and you're not sure what you need, take the time to read this unit – consider it the signposting for your journey to digital heaven! It will give you a brief introduction to the gear you need and then you can turn to the relevant units to find out all about each piece of kit and how to use it. You may, of course, have already bought a computer and know that a Zip drive isn't something that's attached to your trousers. If so you'll probably want to get down to some serious image creations – so go on, skip this bit and head for Unit 9.

The computer

Digital photography centres around the computer. It's often called a workstation, but if Sony hadn't got there first I'd have renamed it the playstation, because digital photography, using a computer to edit images is fun, fun, fun.

The only control most camera users have when creating a photograph is at the camera stage and even then a large proportion of users keep their cameras in automode. The film is then slipped into an envelope and sent to the mail order laboratory to be returned as prints. Often the results are acceptable, but could be better, and that's why many amateur photographers set up their own darkroom – to be in control and produce better results.

The computer is, if you like, the darkroom's replacement. Like a darkroom, the computer lets you crop, resize and enlarge photographs. You can also tone pictures digitally and make the result lighter or darker, but the computer has much more to offer the photographer. You can organise pictures using simple cataloguing software to file and access them with ease. You can use software to enhance the picture either subtly or change the look dramatically. And once the picture's looking just how you want it, you can either store it, print it or share it with others via e-mail or the Internet.

Unlike the darkroom that was, er... dark, the computer sits quite happily on a desk in the spare room. It can also be used for all the other family activities, such as organising those dreaded bills or for the kids to pound the hell out of some evil monster or hurtle around a track in a space-age car.

Once you have a computer at home you will be tempted to hook up to the Internet which opens up a whole world of resources from booking holidays, to sorting out the next mortgage, to buying your tomatoes. The kids can also use it as a reference library or as a source for downloading more games.

In recent years the computer has changed from a gadget that was associated with the nerd who would like to impress you with his programming skills, to an essential purchase alongside the television and washing machine. It's easy to see why. The latest models have operating systems that bleep when you do something

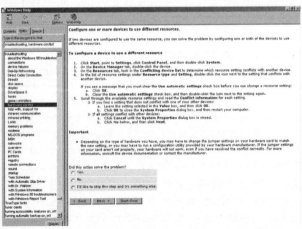

A typical Windows wizard – this particular one guides you through solving a hardware conflict.

wrong and suggest what you should be doing. Some even take over and look after the chores. Gone are the days when you needed a degree just to switch the thing on.

Getting pictures onto the computer

When you've bought a computer you'll have to consider how to get pictures onto it. This is achieved in a number of ways.

The fully digital photographer can use a digital camera to capture pictures electronically. With this sort of camera you don't need film and the results can be downloaded (transferred from the camera via a cable or card) to the computer. Unit 4 explains what types of cameras are available and how you use them to take digital pictures.

You may already have a vast collection of prints, negatives or slides that you'd like to enhance or catalogue. And you may not be ready to invest in a digital camera. You can continue to take photographs using film and invest in a scanner to convert the photographs into digital files.

There are two types of scanner – flatbed models that look like photocopiers and are suitable for prints and flat artwork or film scanners that will look after the negatives strips or mounted slides.

Unit 5 explains what sorts of scanners are available and how you use them to digitise your photographs.

If you can't afford a scanner, don't have the time to scan or want better quality than a home scanner can deliver, you can use the service of a digital lab to process your films and scan them in on a high-quality drum bed scanner. The high quality digital images are then saved on a CD. Photo CD and Picture CD hold images that can be printed up to A4. The disk holds the entire content of your film and comes with an index print so you can see, at a glance, the contents of the CD. The service can also be provided on floppy disk, but quality isn't as good because of the limited storage space.

Some labs will now develop and print your films and store digitised versions on an Internet server that you can access from your computer and download using a modem. For more on this turn to Unit 6.

Editing images

Once a photograph has been loaded onto the computer and is up on screen you can use image-editing software to enhance the picture. This is where the fun begins.

Using image-editing/manipulation programs you can change any element of the picture, altering colour, size, shape, brightness or position of parts of a picture. You can add things, stretch things, lose things – basically the sky's your limit. We'll look at the types of software you can use in Unit 7 and show you how to use it in Units 9, 10 and 11.

Printing your pictures

There's no point in spending time making stunning pictures if you leave them hidden in some directory on the PC. An inkjet printer is what you need. It sits by the computer and allows you to print A4 or A3 pictures, depending on the model you buy, in minutes. You can print on normal paper or a vast range of sticky-backed versions to put on disks, T-shirts and mugs. The home printer can also produce smart business stationery, greetings cards, calendars, newsletters and more.

To find out all about printers turn to Unit 13.

Saving pictures

One problem with digital pictures is that they take up space on the computer. An A4 photo has a file size of around 15 Mb so it doesn't take much to start to fill up your computer's hard disk, especially if you take lots of pictures. Fortunately, the answer's in removable storage. Manufacturers make portable drives that have large capacity removable media. The latest Zip drive holds 250 Mb of data on a disk that takes up just over twice the space of a standard 3¹/₂″ floppy disk.

Most computers come with the option of a CD writer now too. This offers 650 Mb of storage space that is the equivalent of over 460 floppy disks. There are many other options, too, find out more in Unit 14.

Get connected

Hardly a day goes by without a mention of Internet shopping – even children's TV programmes are constantly at you to contact their e-mail address or visit their Web site. The digital photographer can benefit too. Get connected to the Web using a modem and you can source great free programs, extra images, stunning typefaces and the latest hardware drivers to boost your hobby. You could even put your pictures on the Web for everyone to see. All you need is a modem and an ISP. Don't worry – it's all explained in Unit 18.

3 | THE COMPUTER

A computer is the most expensive purchase you'll make when setting up your digital system and it's also the most important part of the outfit. There are many questions that need answering and the most obvious is: 'What do all the specifications mean?'

Specification lists are often daunting and can easily scare the living daylights out of you. Fortunately, we can forget most of it. We need to concentrate on four areas: the processor, memory, graphics card and hard drive. Get these right and the rest is secondary.

The brain

The main component of a computer is the processor, or central processing unit (CPU). This is the computer's brain and its speed is measured in megahertz (MHz), which is an indication of how fast the computer can process information. Many features of image-editing programs require the computer to work hard and you'll find some will slow the computer down, sometimes almost to a grinding halt. Generally speaking, the larger the MHz the faster the computer will work and the less you'll be hanging around waiting for it to finish the job, especially when you work with large images. The latest PCs have 600 MHz, but anything over 300 MHz is acceptable.

The working area

The computer's memory is used to perform tasks and is known as random access memory, or RAM for short. It's measured in megabytes (Mb) and is one of the most important considerations for digital imaging, as it's the part of the computer that programs need in order to run. The computer's operating systems also run from the RAM and they're so complex these days that they often need around 30 Mb before you can even consider opening a program.

Look on the side of any software box and you'll see the minimum requirement to run the program. Microsoft Word needs 20 Mb to be comfortable and Adobe Photoshop needs 64 Mb. RAM is usually one of the first figures quoted on the computer's spec list and most are now sold with 64 Mb as standard, but they can be upgraded.

The computer usually has a couple of spare slots where the user can clip more memory in as required. While RAM used to be very expensive, around £1000 for 64 Mb, it's now selling for around £1 per megabyte so it's worth adding as much as you can afford. Check when you buy the computer what the maximum capacity is. For digital imaging the more the better, so try and equip yourself with at least 128 Mb.

The filing cabinet

The hard drive is like the filing cabinet of the computer where all the programs and files are stored. Most computers now come with at least a 6 gigabyte (Gb) hard drive which is plenty of space for all the programs you're likely to store, but if you intend working with pictures at high resolution this will soon fill up. Fortunately you can buy and install additional hard drives or save your pictures onto removable storage.

Programs such as Photoshop use this area to store parts of the image process when it's working on a big file and it's known as the scratch disk. If there's not much room left you'll see the message, 'Scratch disk full' and you won't be able to continue working on the image until you free up some space.

The eye

Another less obvious but equally important item is the graphics card. The emphasis placed on these in the shops is their ability to cope with the latest games, producing arcade-quality graphics and stunningly fast redraws. But the graphics card has an important role for us, too. The better cards display colours more accurately so what you see on the monitor is what you'll receive from your printer. A graphics card is also responsible for allowing larger monitors to be used. So as you become more serious and decide to upgrade from the standard 17" model to a 21" you have to be sure the card will support it. Like most of the components in the computer this can be upgraded at a later date.

Upgrading

Look around the back of a PC and you'll probably find a series of plates covering gaps in the chassis. These can be removed to make way for other internal components. Open up the case of the computer and you'll see a frighteningly large amount of diodes, circuitry and chips, all housed on a large green board. This is known as the motherboard and is the point at which all the components connect to talk to each other. It's a fragile part of the computer and if you do open the back you should touch the metal of the case to remove any static from your body and ideally wear a static band to avoid any further static build-up, as this can short the circuits.

Just behind the metal plates of the chassis you will find free slots in the motherboard. This is where you can install accessories such as a SCSI card, internal modem, or USB ports if your PC hasn't already got them.

Left: Upgrade your RAM by clipping extra memory into these slots. Right: The PCI slots allow other items to be added such as an inernal modem.

Which type?

When choosing a computer you'll notice that from the outside they all look very similar – a dull beige box with a similarly boring coloured monitor. That is until Apple came along with the iMac – a fun looking model with a rounded body in colours such as tangerine, grape and strawberry. We'll come back to that later, however.

Most shops will automatically try to sell you a computer that's become known as a personal computer (PC). These operate using Microsoft Windows and there's a larger choice of models with the range of software sold in high street stores outnumbering the software available for Macs by about 10 to 1. The Apple Mac was originally designed for graphics and, as such, has a better understanding of colour management to ensure really accurate colours on screen. The iMac has revitalised a falling market share, as it's an attractive design that you'd be happy to put in the family room.

The operating systems are very different. PCs, as mentioned, run on Windows, while Macs have their own unique system. When running a program such as Photoshop you'll hardly notice any difference on either platform. Apart from a few shortcut keys being different, the actions and modes all appear in the same place on screen. The main difference is the file system. A PC file needs an extension at the end of its description. So if you save a picture that you've called baby it needs to be 'baby.jpg' so the PC knows it's a jpeg file. A Mac doesn't need this information.

If you decide on a PC there are dozens of models to choose from and it's hard to know which way to turn. In most cases the main difference is that the chassis is manufactured to a specification requested by the retailer while the components inside are the same whichever machine you buy. What really counts is after-sales service and support. Several magazines have conducted in-magazine surveys to give them lots of facts and figures about reliability, after sales support and ease of use. In these surveys Dan, Dell and Gateway continually win awards of confidence from their readers.

An alternative is a laptop computer, so called because of its portable nature. These offer similar processing power to normal desktop machines, but in a compact book-style casing. The display is obviously smaller, but you can work with images while on your travels. This type of machine needs a rechargeable battery to function away from home and can be connected to the mains when you're back at the office. Most can be fitted with a removable storage drive to back up images, and many have a PCMCIA card reader option so you can input cards from cameras using the relevant adapter. This makes the laptop a practical tool for the press photographer who can take a digital picture, process it on the laptop and then download to the office in a matter of minutes.

Types of connection

Digital image makers have access to dozens of different accessories to help make the most of the subject. These accessories, known in the computer world as peripherals, connect to the processor via cables. Internal versions such as storage devices and internal modems plug straight into the motherboard or link with internal cables while external devices need to be connected to ports around the back of the computer. There are several types of connector that vary depending on the type of product being used and the quantity of data and speed they need to be transferred at. A simple item such as a mouse connects to the serial port which, in the PC's case, is a small oblong, nine-pin socket while on a Mac it's a round eight-pin plug.

Until recently the Mac had a similar sized plug to transfer data to the printer while the PC went for a more elaborate 25-pin connector, known as the parallel printer port. A printer needs data such as image size and colour information so more pins are necessary to transfer the data. It doesn't have to be particularly fast, however, because the info is stored in a buffer and then runs along at the same speed as the print head travels across the paper.

Fast data transfer is preferable when using storage devices, hard drives and CD writers. These are usually connected to a SCSI port. SCSI (pronounced 'skuzzy') can transfer data at much faster speeds to offer, in some cases, almost immediate transfer. The Mac used to have SCSI as standard, but now, like the PC, you have to install a SCSI card on the motherboard to provide a connector in the back of the computer. Adaptec is the biggest name in SCSI boards and it produces a wide range for different needs. Most allow up to seven items to be connected in a chain, a few have the option of up to 14 to be connected, but it's doubtful that many of us would ever need this capacity.

Several versions of SCSI port exist from the original 50-pin to a narrower 50-pin version to a 68-pin version – each offering faster transfer than the previous version. The data transfer rate is also continually being improved with the fastest currently being an Ultra-160, offering 160 Mbs per second transfer speed.

SCSI may be fast but it has always been temperamental. The items in a chain have to be individually numbered and the last one has to have termination to stop signals otherwise it tries to leave the chain. Some hardware drivers conflict with others so you may have a series of items working perfectly and then you install another and things go wrong. There are usually ways around conflicts, but you have to be knowledgeable to be able to find the fault and then rectify it.

One of the main causes is the advanced SCSI programming interface (ASPI) layer. I have had calls from many readers of *Digital PhotoFX* who've struggled to make a film scanner work when they've connected it to the computer and in most cases they had a Zip drive installed too. The problem is that as you load a new bit of hardware it often updates the ASPI layer which might not be compatible with a previous bit of installed gear. Fortunately, in most cases, the correct version can be downloaded from the scanner manufacturer's Web site.

Peripherals using any of the connection methods I've just covered can only be attached and unattached when the computer is switched off. This can be frustrating if it takes around five minutes fully to boot up your PC.

To overcome conflicts and connection problems manufacturers joined forces to develop the universal serial bus (USB), a mini-plug that is a little slower than SCSI, but can then be connected and disconnected while the machine is on. This is known as hot plugging and the computer automatically detects when a device has been plugged in and locates the correct software from the hard drive or asks for it to be installed.

One other system I've not covered is Firewire, or IIE3974 as it's technically known. This was developed by Apple and is much faster than any other form of connector. Unfortunately, only a few hard drives and professional digital camcorders currently use this system.

How to upgrade your existing model

You may have had a PC for several years that could now be beginning to feel the strain as the latest software and peripherals demand power. If you can't see the point in buying a new computer, you may be able to upgrade your existing one. The main part to replace is the processor. At the time of writing, the PC has speeds up to 733 MHz and Apple has speeds up to 500 MHz. Prices of these fall as fast as speeds rise. Some earlier motherboards won't be able to cope with the latest processors, so check before you buy. If the motherboard is too old you can always replace it. Watch costs, however, because it can soon become more beneficial to replace the whole machine.

If you don't have a SCSI connector or USB sockets consider buying an adapter to add these. Make sure the SCSI card is the correct one to cope with the devices you intend using.

Graphics cards come in all shapes and sizes with fancy names such as Blaster Voodoo and Matrox Mystique. The more expensive ones are designed to work with 3D rendering and the latest games. If you're using it for image making buy one that can produce accurate colours. Make sure the graphics card you're considering will support the size of monitor you'll want to use.

Extra memory is a must if you intend working with big image files and don't want to hang around watching the processor crawl along performing a task. It clips into slots on the motherboard. Have a look to see how many slots you have free. Some computers have just one slot free, so buying a small memory chip with the intention of buying more when you can afford it is false economy because you'll have to ditch it when you buy the larger chip.

The monitor

The monitor, or screen, is the part of the computer outfit that displays the image, text, file or program. The basic design, using a cathode ray (CRT), is similar to the household television tube in which a stream of electrons is fired out of a red, green or blue gun from the rear of the funnel-shaped tube. The beam hits a coating of red, green and blue phosphor dots on the inside of the screen making them glow for a fraction of a second. An image is built up as the beam scans across the tube from top to bottom. The speed it takes to do this is known as the refresh rate, measured in hertz. Many of the latest monitors have a refresh rate of 100 Hz which means the screen image is redrawn 100 times every second – impossible for the human eye to detect.

The phosphor dots are arranged in threes or in alternating lines depending on the type of monitor. A shadow mask controls the distance between the phosphors. This thin metal plate has tiny holes that determine where the electron beams fall on the phosphors. The distance between the holes is known as dot pitch and is one of the factors that control image quality. Most of the latest monitors have a dot pitch of 0.28 mm or smaller.

Monitors come in various shapes and sizes, ranging from 15″ desktop size up to huge 22″ designer models; others include LCD panel styles, while some are even built into the computer.

The size of the monitor is misleading. The figure quoted in inches is, like the television, the diagonal measurement of the tube and also includes a small amount that's hidden behind the casing. This may mean a 21″ model, for example, may actually have a viewing width of only about 16″.

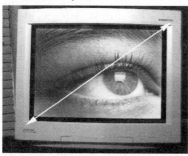

The size of the monitor is measured across its diagonal.

The size is important if you like to view your image magnified and still see the majority of it. It's also easier to display the various palettes down one side of the image so the view isn't cluttered. Some professional image makers buy a special card to power two monitors side by side and have all the toolboxes and palettes on one, leaving the other free for the image, but for most of us that's a little excessive. Choose the biggest you can afford, but beware as the bigger models can take up a huge chunk of your desk space.

The monitor connects to the computer using a standard 15-pin video graphics array (VGA) lead. Some of the latest machines, from the likes of Mitsubishi, also have bayonet nut connectors (BNC). This allows two computers to connect and use the one monitor. The Mitsubishi also has an optional universal serial bus (USB) connector allowing four USB accessories including a printer, scanner and card reader to connect and be used by both computers. You simply switch between the two using a button on the front of the monitor.

One of the more important aspects of a monitor is its resolution that is measured in dots per inch (dpi). PCs have monitors with 96 dpi and Apple Macs have 72 dpi. The size of the monitor determines how many pixels can be displayed at these resolutions. Older 14″ models had a 640 × 480 pixel resolution and are known as VGA monitors, but the newer 17″ monitors have XGA displays giving 1024 × 768 pixels, while the high-end 21″ models offer 1600 × 1200 pixel viewing.

You can adjust some smaller monitors to display this resolution but the information becomes smaller on screen and less comfortable to view. The display can be adjusted from options within the computer's control panel. On a PC it's adjusted using the settings menu from the Display option and on the Apple Mac from the monitors and sound option.

As the resolution figure increases the refresh rate goes down, and the lower this figure becomes the more likely it is that the screen will flicker, especially when it's 75 Hz or slower.

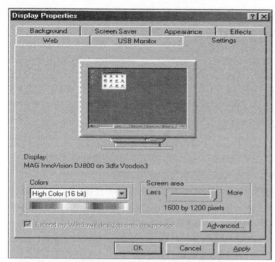

Setting the monitor at different resolutions changes the appearance of icons and folders.

Above and right: At high resolution the text becomes smaller but there's much more room to keep palettes open side by side.

Colour calibration

All monitors have controls to adjust brightness and contrast. You can usually also adjust the way the image appears on screen with pincushion and barrel distortion control to ensure a perfectly shaped picture and horizontal and vertical shift to centre the image.

The most important adjustment is the colour balance. This needs to be accurate to guarantee that what you see on the monitor is what you obtain when you print out the result. Setting up the monitor accurately is a technique known as colour calibration which can be difficult to get right but is well worth the effort.

The problem is that the image viewed on a monitor is red, green, blue (RGB) and uses projected light, while the printed output is cyan, magenta, yellow, black (CMYK) and viewed using reflected lighting. We can do a few things to ensure this doesn't get in the way, however.

The first thing to note is that the colour balance of a monitor changes as it warms up. So don't try to attempt accurate colour calibration unless the monitor's been switched on for at least half an hour. It's also beneficial if the room you're viewing the monitor in has consistent lighting. A room that's used in the day, with viewing in window light, and at night, under tungsten lighting, will make the screen image look different in each case. Try to balance this out by using a daylight bulb for evening viewing, or use a blind to block out daylight.

The background desktop colour, known as wallpaper on a PC, can also influence our eyes. Try to keep it a neutral colour and plain, as loud colours and patterns can affect reality. Similarly, coloured walls will affect the image on screen – once again working in a room with neutral coloured walls is best.

Some image-editing programs, such as Adobe Photoshop, have monitor-calibration software supplied. This is used to adjust the brightness and contrast followed by the gamma to give an optimised display. You simply open the control panel and follow the on-screen instructions.

Don't work with a picture as a wallpaper image – it's not only distracting but may also make it difficult to spot desktop icons.

Most monitors have a custom profile that should be selected first. The monitor profile will set the recommended white point, phosphors and gamma, but these can usually be set manually if you don't have the correct profile. The white point is the colour temperature of the screen, phosphors is the type of screen used in your monitor and gamma is the brightness range. Setting a low gamma value of, say, 0.8 will darken the printed image, while a high value of 3.0 will compensate for a dark screen image. The default is usually around 1.8.

You can usually also set the temperature of the ambient lighting you're working in, which adjusts the monitor brightness to compensate for dim or bright room conditions.

Another method of calibration is to create a test print. Pick an image with plenty of colours and neutral tones and make a print.

Then view the print at the side of the monitor. Compare the two for colour balance, brightness, contrast and saturation, then adjust the monitor, making notes of the adjustments, so that the image on screen matches what you've printed out. Now revert to the original monitor settings and apply a reverse set of corrections to the printer's software. If the monitor needed to be lightened to match the printed output the printer setting obviously needs to be darkened to match the monitor. Similarly, a cyan cast removed from the monitor needs to be added in the printer's properties. Get the idea? Now your prints will look more like the image on screen.

Holding a print in front of the same image on a monitor helps you assess whether the screen is calibrated correctly.

Mouse

All on-screen actions are performed using your hand on a small control, known, oddly, as a mouse. These come in all shapes and sizes but the general principle remains the same. The on-screen cursor is moved around when you move a ball inside the mouse. The ball touches contacts and sends the cursor around the screen. Some have the ball underneath the mouse that is moved around on a mouse pad. Others have the ball on top controlled using a finger or thumb.

All mice have at least one button that you click to select menu items or perform tasks. PCs have two buttons, expressed as left and right – left click here, right click there. Some of the latest mice have up to four buttons that can be assigned different tasks, one may be to open files, another to double-click, another to save files. You usually have the option of customising the mouse to perform certain tasks on each button.

Another option that is more suitable for digital imaging is a graphics tablet. This has a pen as a replacement to the mouse that seems more natural when drawing or selecting round objects. The pen can also be used with painting programs to create works of art, especially when used with packages such as Painter that has various oils and watercolour paints and many brush styles.

One other option that's becoming popular for word processing is voice-activated devices that can open and close files and even type out letters without your having to go near a mouse. Currently, these won't do everything needed for the image maker, so avoid the temptation.

4 | TAKING A DIGITAL PICTURE

In this unit we will look first at the types of digital camera that are available and explain their features. We'll then look at the differences between using a digital camera and a film-based model, and follow on with ways to approach typical subjects that you'll encounter as a digital photographer.

Types of digital camera

The digital camera market has developed dramatically since Casio launched the QV-10 in February 1995. This was the first mass-market model, but, like all technology-based products, costs have dropped considerably and specifications have risen at an equally fast rate so the Casio looks decidedly primitive by today's standards. The new digital camera market can be divided into several categories (see colour plate 2).

You'd be hard pushed to find a model as basic as that original Casio, with its 320 × 240 pixel CCD. The new basic or entry-level model has a minimum of 640 × 480 pixel resolution and is known as a VGA model – short for video graphics array. These are fine for creating pictures that will only be viewed on the computer monitor, which has a similar 640 × 480 pixel display, or for producing very small pictures to appear in print. If you're considering digital photography as a means to illustrate your Web site, one of these camera will be adequate; otherwise avoid them.

The next step up is XGA, or extended graphics array, which has 1024 × 768 pixel resolution and is designed to cope with larger, higher resolution monitors. This type of camera will also allow good-quality prints to be made up to the standard 4 × 6 inch enprint that you normally get back from your film processor. It's fine for the occasional photographer who records family parties/holidays, but the enthusiast will need better and this is where megapixel models deliver.

A megapixel camera is the lowest resolution an enthusiast photographer would be satisfied with to replace an existing 35 mm camera. This type of camera has a CCD with over one million pixels giving an actual picture taking resolution of 1280 × 1024 pixels. This ensures a very good 5 × 7 inch print and, at a push, an A4 enlargement.

But it's the latest breed of super-megapixel cameras that provides the really interesting area to look at. Some, for example, the Nikon Coolpix 990, can produce A4 pictures that are hard to distinguish from 35 mm. Many users have pushed this type of camera to its limits and even get satisfactory A3 pictures from the 2048 × 1536 pixel CCD. This type of camera has really opened up the digital market and is the segment that's currently developing most rapidly. Even so the three million-plus pixel resolution is still a far cry from the 14 million pixel resolution that a 35 mm negative is estimated to produce.

A couple of models from Sony and Fuji have single-lens reflex viewing that use a series of mirrors to reflect the light that comes through the lens to the optical viewfinder. The advantage of an SLR is that it's more accurate, because you see exactly what the lens sees when taking a picture. The downside is that they're bulky compared with the compact style of the non-SLR.

The next category is based on existing 35 mm SLRs. While most only have up to three million pixels resolution, they handle like conventional cameras and offer the same range of features, including interchangeable lenses and speed of use. The problem is cost. At the time of writing the lowest priced model cost well over £2,000. You'd have to be serious to use one of these, or a professional, who can cover the cost via commissions.

The prime category is, once again, in the realm of the professional. There are several backs that fit onto medium-format cameras such as the Bronica or Hasselblad. These scan across the film area and give the highest resolution of all current digital cameras. The Megavision T3, for example, features a 2048 × 2048 pixel CCD that shoots at up to one frame per second offering a four million pixel resolution and produces stunning results for advertising and fashion photographers.

There are two other types of camera worth mentioning but I won't go into too much detail, as the quality of pictures they produce isn't good enough for making prints. Video grabbers sell for around £70 and are designed for conferencing. Each user connects one to his computer and as they communicate using e-mail or Internet their picture can be seen by the others in the conference. This type of camera can be used to make still frames but the quality is usually only 320 pixels resolution.

Digital camcorders are fantastic products for capturing moving images to be used in presentations or for impressive Web creations, but, once again, quality rarely exceeds 640 pixels so the image isn't good enough for making enlargements. You do, however, have access to over 90,000 images on one tape so you're more or less guaranteed that decisive moment.

To calculate whether the camera you're considering is capable of producing images of a suitable size divide the cameras quoted pixel measurements by the desired output resolution. So, for example, a camera with a 1024 × 768 pixel CCD will produce a 5 × 4 inch print from a 200 dpi inkjet printer – 1024/200 × 768/200. There's nothing to stop you making bigger pictures, but you may start to see jagged edges on closer inspection (see Table 4.1)

Camera type	Web/screen viewing 72 dpi	Inkjet print 200 dpi	Magazine repro 300 dpi
640 × 480	9 × 7″	3.2 × 2.4″	2.1 × 1.6″
1024 × 768	14 × 10.5″	5 × 4″	3.4 × 2.6″
1280 × 1024	18 × 14″	6.4 × 5″	4.2 × 3.4″
1600 × 1200	22.2 × 16.7″	8 × 6″	5.3 × 4.3″
2048 × 1536	28.4 × 21.3″	10.2 × 7.6″	6.8 × 5.1″

Table 4.1 What maximum print size can I obtain at optimum quality?

Digital camera features explained

Few digital cameras have strayed from the conventional camera shape. After all it's a tried and tested formula, so why change? Looking at the camera from the front you'll see the lens positioned around the middle area and, if one's integral, a flash to one side. In most cases the user looks through a separate viewfinder to compose the picture and takes the shot with the shutter release that's positioned above the right hand finger on top of the camera.

The liquid crystal display (LCD)

Many cameras also have a large LCD panel round the back of the body that can also be used as a viewfinder. The advantage of this is that the image you see on screen is what the camera's lens is seeing, so it's more accurate to use than the optical finder that's positioned to the side of the lens. The disadvantage (and there always seems to be one) is that the LCD guzzles batteries.

Manufacturers are slowly getting round this problem by providing daylight assisted LCD illumination and higher capacity batteries, but it's still a concern. The best thing to do is to use the LCD only when essential or buy a couple of packs of rechargeable batteries. The LCD can also be used to view pictures you've just taken. This is a great feature to prevent poor pictures being saved because you can edit as you go along, deleting unwanted pictures and saving storage space. The downside is it's another drain on the batteries!

Many cameras have an LCD panel that's used as a viewfinder, but it can also be used to review pictures you've just taken.

The lens

One of the key words in digital photography is resolution – everyone talks about it as though it's some mystical solution to their prayers. But resolution is usually only talked about in terms of the number of pixels on the CCD, and it's something I've used earlier to illustrate the various camera price points. There is, however, no point in having a super-duper resolution CCD if the lens has the optical quality of a milk bottle! And this is one reason why it's worth trusting a traditional camera manufacturer, such as Nikon and Olympus, to produce the sharper lens. They've been making camera lenses for decades and understand what is needed from a lens to make it deliver pictures so sharp that you could almost cut your finger on them.

Like traditional film-based cameras, digital cameras employ the lens to focus the light reflected from the subject onto the CCD to record the photograph. The size the subject appears on the CCD is determined by the focal length of the lens.

Lenses can be split into several groups with the common descriptions: standard, wide-angle, telephoto and zoom.

The standard lens is a close representation of the human eye and has a focal length of around 6 mm. Any lens with a focal length shorter than this, such as 4 mm, is classed as a wide-angle. This lens group gives less magnification than a standard lens, but has a wider field of view so it's useful for photographing subjects such as landscapes, groups, buildings and interiors where a standard lens would crop off important detail at the edges of the scene.

A telephoto lens magnifies the subject, but has a narrower angle of view. This type of lens has a focal length longer than a standard lens, such as 15 mm, and is ideal when photographing subjects from a distance. A telephoto gives a tighter crop and suits subjects such as nature, portraits, candids and sports.

A zoom lens combines a continuous range of focal lengths in one lens that can be changed by altering the distance of individual elements within the optical construction. Some zooms are classed as standard zooms and cover a focal length range around the standard lens. A telezoom offers a range of magnifying focal lengths and the wide-zoom offers a choice of, you guessed it, wide-angle focal lengths.

Beware of cameras with digital zoom lenses. This type of zoom works by magnifying the image from the middle of the CCD so it uses fewer pixels to make the image. You can just as easily do this back home on the computer.

If you're familiar with 35 mm technology you may now be wondering why the 6 mm standard lens isn't an ultra-wide – in 35 mm terms this would normally be classed as a fish-eye and would capture over 180° field of view. The reason for this is simple. The lens on a digital camera is positioned close to the CCD, and is much smaller than film and, as a result, the digital camera focal length is between 1/5 and 1/7 that of the 35 mm camera's equivalent. The physical size of the CCD also limits how wide the focal length of the lens can be and the current limit is, in 35 mm film based terms, 28 mm, which is far less versatile.

Each white frame signifies an increase in lens magnification that enlarges the central area and crops out the surrounds.

Bolt-ons

Jessops sell lenses to fit on the front of a digital camera's lens to convert it to either wider angle or telephoto. Ideally, the camera should have a filter thread to allow the converter to be attached firmly, but many don't so companies such as SRB make adapters to suit most cameras. A few manufacturers also produce slide copiers that attach to the front of the lens and have a holder for a mounted slide. This type of product relies on the camera having a decent macro mode.

Focusing

Most digital cameras have autofocus lenses. The camera will fire an infrared beam at the subject to determine how far away from the camera it is and the information is used automatically to adjust the lens to make the picture sharp. Infrared autofocusing is fine in most conditions but can easily be fooled by glass or subjects out of range of the infrared beam. If you try to shoot through a window it will think that you're focusing on the window glass and the resultant photograph will be blurred. Camera manufacturers get round this in several ways. The obvious answer is to switch to manual focus. Some models give you a full range of distances to select from, others have an infinity button.

The infinity mode sets the camera's focus to the longest distance so you can take pictures through glass without it being fooled.

More advanced cameras will use phase-detection focusing that looks at the subject's contrast to determine its distance. This method of focusing is much more accurate at all distances, but relies on the subject having good contrast, so it's easily fooled in low contrast light. It also struggles on fast-moving objects.

The focusing point of a camera is usually the centre of the frame, which is fine if the subject you want sharp is also in the middle. For off-centre subjects, first point at the subject positioned in the centre of the frame and press the shutter release halfway down to activate and lock focus. Keep holding the release at the halfway point and recompose before pressing the shutter release fully down to take the picture.

Left: Most cameras focus in the centre of the picture that would result in this shot being out of focus. Middle: Use the focus to lock on one of the people and with it held recompose to take a sharper picture. Right: There, that's much better.

Macro mode

Having a lens so close to the CCD does have its benefits and the close-up capabilities of most digital cameras, using the macro mode, is superb. With many models you can get as close as 10 cm but cameras such as the Olympus C-2500 Zoom and Nikon Coolpix 990 allow focusing as close as 2 cm. And at this distance you can fill the frame with subjects the size of a postage stamp. Most macro modes have to be set manually to override the usual 20 cm to infinity autofocus range. It appears as a flower icon on the LCD panel.

The flower icon signifies the macromode.

The close-up mode is perfect for subjects such as flowers.

Flash

An integral flash is a useful addition to ensure good results in low light. If you take a picture indoors, or at night, the camera will detect that the result will be dark and automatically switch the flash on. The flash will then fire when you take the photograph. This is fine if you want to use flash, but sometimes the natural light of a sunset or street illuminations is what you want to capture and flash will destroy the effect. Fortunately, most cameras have several modes to override auto. You can usually switch the flash off for the sunsets; or force it to fire in daylight to add a fill-in which will reduce shadows in harsh sunlight; or red-eye mode that fires a pre flash to reduce the subjects pupils and the harsh red-eye effect.

The power of the flash is quoted in the specifications and usually allows pictures to be taken at distances up to about three metres. Some cameras have a flash sync socket so studio flash can be connected and used for more controlled flash lighting.

You can also use a slave flashgun to introduce lighting effects.

If you switch the flash off be careful of camera shake introduced when the shutter stays open to record the low light. More about this later.

Other features to look out for

Date and time mode

Records the date and time on the picture.

Sound recording

Lets you add audio captions to your pictures.

Black & white and sepia modes

These effects can be created easily in the computer so there seems little point in worrying about these modes.

Self-timer

Delays the shutter firing for around ten seconds giving ample time for the user to run in front of the camera and be included in a group shot. This can also be used to prevent camera shake when the camera's mounted on a tripod.

An interval timer

A useful feature that takes a shot at pre-set intervals so you can leave the camera set up to record varying cloud formations, a flower opening or the changes in a busy street, for example.

Frames

Adds a frame around the subject in camera.

Caption

Adds a caption to the picture.

Negative

Turns the picture into a negative effect – why you'd want to do this is beyond me!

Exposure Compensation

Use this to override the camera's automatic exposure – usually in half-stop steps.

Left: Picture taken on the camera's automatic exposure setting. Middle: With +1.5 exposure compensation. Right: With –1.5 stops exposure compensation

Panorama/Stitch mode

Helps you line up and shoot a series of pictures side by side that can then be joined to make an elongated panoramic image.

Exposure modes

Earlier models were limited to fully automatic exposure systems, but recently models have started to appear with various program modes and overrides. If you want to be more creative choose a model with aperture or shutter priority – you'll see why on page 38.

Memory

When the CCD captures a digital picture it's processed and stored in the camera's memory. The size of the memory determines how many pictures can be stored. Basic cameras have a small memory capacity of around 2 Mb that restricts the number of pictures you can take before it's full. You reuse the memory by downloading the stored pictures onto the computer to make space for new ones.

This method of storage is really restrictive, especially if you want to take a lot of pictures and don't have the chance to save them to the PC. To overcome this manufacturers introduced cameras that use removable memory cards.

Removable memory cards

As with most new technologies several types of product have been introduced and each claims to be the best. The main two are SmartMedia and CompactFlash. SmartMedia has the advantage of being wafer thin so the products it's used in, including mobile phones, can benefit from also being the most compact in their class. The disadvantage is the camera has to have a controller built in so, as newer higher capacity cards are introduced, they won't work in older cameras unless the camera's service department looks after it. The cards are also flimsy and are easily damaged. The highest memory on SmartMedia is currently 64 Mb, although Samsung is working on a one gigabyte card.

CompactFlash is a more substantial card with already higher memory capacity, currently up to 256 Mb. All the processing data are held within the card so it's backward compatible and cameras can accept any size.

In 1981, Sony introduced the floppy disk. Now, nearly two decades later, they're back with a new method of storage, known as the Memory Stick, which is currently sold in sizes up to 64 Mb. This is currently available for use in Sony's digital still and video cameras, and can also be used in a PCMCIA adapter or floppy disk adapter.

The PCMCIA card has been around the longest and is used mostly by professionals in the pro-spec SLR cameras.

Iomega, the company famous for the Zip drive, has introduced the clik! drive which holds 40 Mb of info and connects to the camera to run alongside it.

Finally, the most interesting development is IBM's Micro Drive – a hard drive with a storage space of 340 Mb that is small enough to fit into a camera. Several models currently accept the Micro Drive.

The whole market can be confusing and we may end up in the old Betamax/VHS scenario. If this happens, my money's on CompactFlash and Memory Stick being the VHS with SmartMedia and clik! ending up with the same fate as Betamax.

How to use a digital camera

Digital photography is, in many ways, no different from conventional photography. While the way we capture, enhance and store pictures is far removed, the general principles still exist. To take a digital picture you have to point the camera at the subject and hold it steady. You should consider composition, and careful focusing is still important to ensure your pictures appear sharp. Many of the problems you encounter can be rectified in the computer, but that's no reason to be complacent at the taking stage.

The first thing you need to decide when taking a digital picture is what image quality mode to shoot in and most digital cameras have a variety of options. The obvious choice is the highest resolution, after all that's probably why you picked that particular model in the first place.

This is not always the best option, however. Let's take the Canon PowerShot Pro 70 as an example – it has five options. The highest quality is a raw setting. This saves the picture at the camera's maximum resolution of 1536 × 1024 pixels, and it doesn't compress the file that has a size of 1940 Kb.

The next option is to capture the same number of pixels but the image is saved as a JPEG high quality compressed file. This reduces the image to 360 Kb while normal quality compression makes the file even smaller at 180Kb. You can also use the camera in small mode and save a 768 × 512 image in high-quality JPEG at 140 Kb or a normal quality of just 70 Kb.

The advantage of shooting in raw mode is that you obtain the highest quality pictures. But you can only take one picture on a 4 Mb CompactFlash card. In most cases you're better to go for the finest quality JPEG that still produces a good image, but raises the number of pictures you can take to ten. Saving at the smaller 768 × 512 and normal JPEG quality gives you the opportunity to shoot 47 pictures.

If you're lucky the camera will offer a choice of exposure modes. Program or full auto is often the only option and in this mode you basically just point and shoot. The advantage of having, say, shutter priority is that you can control the shutter speed which is useful if you want to freeze action or make the subject blurred to give a sense of movement. Having aperture priority lets you control the aperture and the amount of sharpness in the scene. This is useful if you want to throw a background out of focus or, alternatively, stop the lens down to gain maximum quality.

Some cameras take the program mode a stage further by including subject-based programs. These include landscape, portrait, sports and close-up modes and the camera ensures the best combination of the aperture and shutter speed is selected for the chosen mode.

Now you're ready to take a picture. Decide whether you're going to use the optical viewfinder or the LCD. Avoid overusing the LCD so your batteries last longer. The only time you really need to use the LCD is for close-ups to avoid a little problem known as parallax error. This happens because your view through the optical finder is offset from the lens and as you move closer to the subject the view becomes more inaccurate. It's easy to chop the top off the scene accidentally or to include some that you didn't want!

As you press the shutter release the camera focuses and confirms this with a light in the viewfinder or an audible signal. When you see or hear this press the shutter release fully down, holding the camera steady to avoid camera shake.

If the camera has an LCD panel you can then switch from record to play and view the result. You have to bear in mind that the picture on the LCD may look sharper than it actually is, which will show up when you enlarge the image on the computer monitor.

If the picture looks okay, revert to record mode and continue taking pictures. If it's bad, press the delete button to remove the image. Watch out here – there's usually an option to delete a single picture or the entire contents, which can't be undone. You're often asked if you're sure you want to continue with a particular action, making it difficult to go wrong. There's often an option to add a protection to individual images to prevent them being deleted, and a thumbnail view that displays nine images on the LCD. Some cameras have a slide show mode so you can run through the contents of the card.

When you return home you can download the pictures onto the computer. There are several ways of doing this and the most common (but slowest) method is to use a cable connected to the computer's serial port or USB socket.

Camera connected to a computer using a cable.

Piccolo detects that a CD or floppy disk has been inserted and automatically shows the picture content on the screen.

Cameras come with special utility software that lets you control the camera from the computer. Once connected you load the software and click on acquire. The program then locates the camera and downloads thumbnail sheets of images stored in its memory. You can then select the pictures you want to download at full resolution. A good optional software program for digital camera users is Piccolo, made by the Digital Camera Company. This locates all the pictures used, recognizes the make of camera they were taken on and then displays them as thumbnails. You can select an individual image, crop it, adjust brightness, contrast and sharpness and save it in one of a variety of formats.

Photos can be enlarged and edited in Piccolo.

A faster way to get pictures onto the computer is to use a card reader that acts like another drive on your desktop. Insert the card into the reader and you have instant access to your pictures. Readers connect either into the printer port or using USB. Some are multi-format models that will accept SmartMedia, CompactFlash and PCMCIA cards.

The third and latest method is by using infrared. You attach a receiver on the computer and just point the camera at it – a cable-free world is approaching!

Digital camera-created pictures always have obscure numbering systems for the images so it's worth renaming them so they make sense. It's also worth backing up the pictures on a Zip disk or CD – if your computer crashes and you lose the lot your memories will be gone forever.

Now you have the basic idea of how to use a digital camera let's look in more detail at the types of subject you can shoot and ways of getting around any limitations the digital camera has.

Photographing people

Look at the prints churning out of the processing machine at your local one hour lab and I guarantee most of the pictures will be of the family. It's the number one subject whether it's romantic pictures of the partner or playful images of the children, granny's 80th birthday, daughter's wedding, son's graduation, first birthday party, school reunion… the list goes on.

The family album is one of the most popular reasons why photos are taken.

Our lives are full of events and the camera is the ideal visual notebook that records these precious moments in time so you can look back on them in years to come.

It's a shame that most of the pictures taken are snaps – point-and-shoot pictures with little care taken in anything other than grabbing the moment. They're good for the record, but we can do better. Here are a few ideas and techniques to improve your family album.

Portraiture

Take a little extra care when photographing individuals. Use the viewfinder to ensure you fill the frame with the head and shoulders for impact. For this sort of composition it's useful if your digital camera has a zoom lens. A focal length of around 90 mm is perfect at delivering flattering perspective. In digital terms this will be specified as between 16–18 mm depending on the camera used. When you use the lens in this range you'll find the background may be thrown slightly out of focus which, in turn, helps make the person stand out.

Portrait mode sets the camera up so it performs best when taking a head and shoulders photo.

If you've been asked to produce a set of pictures for a model's portfolio, care with background is important. Subtle shades and harmonious colours will help lift the model from any distractions. If the person you're photographing is close to the background ask her to step forward to help reduce its sharpness.

Another option is to include some of the background when you want to show the person in character. A colleague from the office by her desk or shop assistant by his products, for example, will

Avoid cluttered background when shooting a portrait.

make more imaginative photographs. Here you really need a wider angle lens and, in a digital camera's case, something around 6 mm is fine. If you can't get the whole setting in the frame either step back or, where possible, consider buying a wide-angle lens that goes over the front of your camera's lens.

Try asking the model to hold props or use a background that's appropriate to the subject.

Don't make the picture look too static or false, capturing people in action, or just as they look at you, will look better than a frozen smile. Using props can help make the subject comfortable; something to lean on or sit on will prevent a restless pose.

Whatever type of portrait you take one of the most important considerations is making sure the person you're about to photograph is looking relaxed. Make them at ease by friendly conversation; the less anxious they feel, the more relaxed and natural your photographs will look. It's much easier when you're working with someone you know, but once a stranger is involved a little extra effort beforehand makes all the difference.

If you're taking the photographs for your own portfolio, project or for your stock library try sketching a few ideas to show the subject what you have in mind. This makes it easier to ensure you're both on the same wavelength when poses are being arranged.

Sketch some rough drawings to help the model understand what you're after.

It's also a good idea to look through books or magazines and pick out examples that will work well. An important note here is to choose your model to suit the pose you want to create – don't try to recreate an idea with the wrong person; it will never work.

Another superb benefit of a digital camera with an LCD preview is being able to show the person the photograph you've just taken. This not only gives them an idea of what you're trying to achieve but will make them relax even more if they are impressed with the results. It's also useful to know whether they're happy with what you're creating rather than wasting money printing results that are disappointing.

Children

Children and animals – the photographer's nightmare. But they don't have to be. There are techniques we can apply to help keep your kids happy as you fiddle around with camera settings and props.

As your children grow from babies into teenagers, the way they react to the camera will change, through several stages. Manage these stages and you'll create a fantastic record of them growing up.

At pre-crawling stage babies won't be particularly aware of the camera and can't go anywhere. So the only thing you have to consider is how to get them into a comfortable and relaxed position. Try using a couple of cushions to either side to provide support and use a rattle or squeaky toy to keep their attention. Avoid using flash too much – it may be frightening at such a young age.

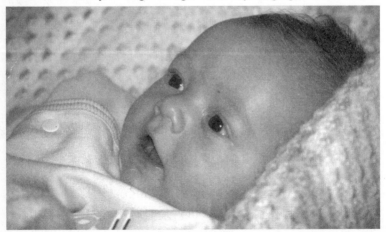

The easiest time to photograph babies is at the pre-crawling stage.

Keeping babies still for a photo session once they start to crawl can be a nightmare. This is the stage of life that's the hardest to manage and the best option is to find something that will keep them amused while you take the photos.

A contented child means you have more chance of getting a picture that you like, and one of the best ways of achieving this equilibrium is to let them get on with what they're doing while you photograph them as they play. Photographing children in this way is a great opportunity to capture all kinds of emotion from surprise to sadness, amusement to anger.

As your children start to walk and learn to talk they also develop minds of their own and you have to be more patient and understanding. If you've been taking pictures regularly they'll be used to the camera and won't mind having a picture taken, but shyness and stubbornness can develop, so be prepared to explain why you want to take pictures and offer a treat if they co-operate. Don't force them or you'll end up with a mardy kid who simply won't co-operate.

Take pictures of kids at parties when they're preoccupied with what's going on around them.

The birthday party is the ideal occasion for photography. While the children are engrossed in unwrapping presents you can get on with the photography and capture the ever-changing expressions. Try photographing the moment the candles on the cake are blown out. Switch the camera flash off and you'll get a lovely natural light glow to the faces as they blow. This can be enhanced in the computer if the exposure is not as good as you'd have liked.

If you want a more posed picture with the child looking at the camera try a little trick I stumbled on. Tell them that there's a little gnome/fairy who runs around inside the camera lens making sure the camera will work when the picture is taken. Even if they're old enough not to believe you they'll still look into the lens and you'll get the perfect shot.

If you decide to have a session with studio lighting make sure you have everything set up beforehand to prevent boredom setting in as you fiddle about moving lights and taking flash readings. Only a few digital cameras can be used successfully with studio lighting. Make sure it has aperture control so you can stop the lens down to avoid overexposure. If the camera doesn't have a flash sync socket you can use the built-in flash to trigger the studio lights by placing some infrared filter gel over the flash. This will trigger the slave flash of the studio light without affecting the picture.

Some digital cameras now have flash sync sockets to trigger studio flash.

Choose props carefully – an uncomfortable seat will make children fidget. A beanbag always seems to keep kids happy and can make a colourful backdrop.

As they develop into teenagers you'll be able to photograph them while they indulge in their hobbies: riding horses, playing football, riding bikes. Take an interest in their hobby and they'll be less bothered when you start to poke your lens into their space.

Whatever they're involved in, catching kids in action is usually easier than asking them to pose.

As mentioned in the portrait section, being able to see a digital camera picture instantly has a major benefit when photographing children. It's like magic to youngsters and it usually makes them want to be photographed again and again.

Candids

Candid pictures can make great alternatives to portraits. The unaware subject will obviously be more naturally engaged in everyday life as you take the shot. This doesn't give you artistic licence to disrespect the person's privacy, however. It might seem normal for paparazzi to invade privacy, but how would you like it if you were the subject of the invasion? Be respectful, ask the person's permission to take some pictures and if they're okay with this let them get on with whatever they're doing while you take the pictures. Avoid wide-angle lenses and use a telephoto to keep a distance then you're less obviously poking your nose into their affairs. Keep the camera up to your eye and wait for the right moment to take the picture.

Taking candid pictures of people when they aren't aware produces much more natural results.

Alternatively if you can't pluck up courage to ask permission, use the camera at waist level and take pictures discreetly. Switch the flash off to avoid obvious picture taking. Cameras with a swivel viewfinder are perfect for this type of photography as they enable you to compose the picture with the camera at waist height or above your head. Great candid pictures capture great moments, great expressions and great poses.

Using flash

In all forms of people pictures watch out when using flash – the harshness can sometimes make skin go deathly white. This may be okay if you have a vampire for a friend, but otherwise it's a disaster. Come to think of it, having a vampire as a friend wouldn't exactly be a bed of roses! The harshness is often caused because of the background.

A digital camera's built-in flash can cause the face to look washed out. This can be corrected in the brightness and contrast settings of the image-editing software.

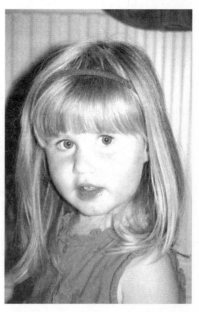

The camera's metering system may be fooled into kicking out three metres, worth of flash to reach a background when your subject may be just one metre away. With built-in flash there's not a lot you can do about this problem because few digital cameras have flash exposure compensation.

If the room is reasonably bright your best way forward is to switch the flash off and rely on the ambient light. Cameras can detect colour casts from artificial lighting and compensate using their auto white-balance controls. The only problem you'll have then is if the artificial light is low. In such cases the camera will use a slow shutter speed and the result may suffer from camera shake and appear blurred. Hold the camera steady either by supporting your body against a wall or by resting your arms on a table. Take a deep breath just before you press the shutter release, and don't stab at the release – try to get into the habit of gently squeezing it down.

Pets

There are few cats or dogs that will sit still while you point your lens at them. You may spend ages getting them to sit still but as soon as you step back and raise the camera they come running up to you. The best option is to get someone else to stroke them and move quickly out of frame as you press the shutter release. It's easy to tempt a kitten to roll around with a ball of wool or cuddly toy and, if your reactions are quick you'll get some decent results. Tempting a dog to a chewing stick will also allow time to take a few pictures. Spend a little time grooming the pet before you take the shot so its coat has a lovely sheen and avoid flash. Pets' eyes become glowing green balls when flash is used.

Fluff was half asleep so it wasn't difficult to take this shot.

Landscapes

Look on the walls of most houses and you'll often see pictures of either the family or a great landscape. In most cases these landscape pictures are paintings created by the likes of Turner, Constable or Monet – each with their own perspective on a scene. With a digital camera you can capture the scene as nature intended or, with the aid of a computer, enhance or distort the truth to suit your artistic viewpoint.

Mention landscape photography and the name Ansel Adams may spring to mind. While he didn't have access to the computer he did have the skills needed to turn a standard scene into a spectacular image using darkroom skills. His black & whites, shot on large-format cameras, gave so much depth to the pictures that you almost felt you were in the scene.

So what is it about landscape photography that makes it such a popular subject? For starters there's the emotional side. It's an opportunity to be alone and reflect on the stressful day in the office or hectic home life. It is, if you like, the chance to pamper yourself with a bit of self-therapy. But you also have the benefit of being able to keep fit while walking and enjoying the fresh air.

Another reason why so many landscape pictures are taken is that they act as a record of that once-in-a-lifetime holiday, or the stunning waterfall, spooky forest or colourful valley. Take a little care over the composition and exposure and you could hang these memories on the wall.

The definition of a landscape varies from person to person. Some would say that it has to include lots of elements as a scenic view, but my definition would allow even a single tree silhouetted against a sky or a lone mushroom with a background of grass to fit the category. We can even include buildings in this category and call it an industrial landscape. What's important is not so much the subject, or equipment used, but more the lighting and time of day.

If you stayed in the same location for a whole day you'd see that scene transform many times as the sun passes across the sky. See the early morning mist, offset against a soft blue sky; through to harsh midday sky with its high contrast; on to glowing orange colours as the sun sets; and finally, the cold blue light of the moon.

And that's without the variable weather conditions that can have a major impact on the scene. One day may be overcast and look about as exciting as one of John Major's suits, yet another day the sun's rays may be crashing across the scene creating a tapestry of colour. It's all about being in the right place at the right time.

The time of year also affects the look of the land. A spring scene may include a bank of lush green trees, while in autumn the same scene will be a fiery red, and in winter it could be covered in a blanket of snow.

Revisit the scene

Plan your visit, but don't be afraid to give up and try again on a different day if the weather isn't right. Try visiting the same scene at different times of the day to see what effect the position the sun has on the land. You'll be surprised what an effect the position of the sun can have on the scene. At midday the shadows are harsh and compressed below the subject yet morning and evening produce softer and longer shadows that can sweep across the scene giving added depth and interest.

Set yourself a project to photograph the same scene either several times throughout the day or year and mount the results side by side in a frame or album.

A wide-angle lens is a better choice for landscapes as it allows you to capture more of the scene. Watch out for large expanses of sky that can make the picture look empty and often boring. Also take care with exposure in such situations, the sky can cause the camera to underexpose the ground, creating a vast expanse of dark tones. If your camera has an exposure lock, point it at the ground first and lock the exposure before recomposing.

Don't dismiss the telephoto lens – use this to home in on one area of the scene such as a silhouetted tree, babbling brook or a bank of sand dunes. Tight framing of such subjects can lead to dramatic results.

Tips

As digital cameras tend to drain the power out of batteries quickly always carry a spare set or two. There's nothing worse than reaching a location, taking a few shots and then seeing the power signal on replace if you haven't a spare pack to pop in.

Try to ensure there's some foreground detail to lead you into a landscape picture.

Watch for the weather. Digital cameras, being totally reliant on electronics can be very temperamental if they become damp. If you do intend shooting in the rain or mist think about buying a waterproof housing.

Take a small tripod like the Ultrapod to hold the camera steady and prevent camera shake in low light. Use this with a digital camera that has aperture control and you can really make the most of the depth of field by shooting with small apertures.

The Ultrapod is a superb little tabletop tripod that can also be attached to a tree branch or fence post.

Shoot pictures with the intention of adding elements together using your image-editing software. An overhanging tree branch can be used to frame a photo that has an uninspiring foreground, while a blue sky, scattered with white clouds, can pump life into a picture that comes out with a dull grey sky. Always take care that the lighting on each component matches. A silhouetted tree will look strange when added to a front-lit scene!

Architecture

How many times have you tried to photograph a building and it's either so big that you can't fit it all in the viewfinder, or you turn up on that once in a lifetime visit to find the sacred temple or cathedral covered in scaffolding? It happens. Many of the things that would have ruined a good photograph can now thankfully be rectified with a little skill on the computer, which I'll cover in later units.

There are, however, several things you can do to improve a photograph of a building before it reaches the computer. As with most subjects that are photographed outdoors the time of day makes all the difference between a good and bad picture.

Some buildings look as dull as dishwater when photographed on an overcast day. Having the sun illuminating the subtle textures of stone brings out golden shades, emphasises depth and creates almost three-dimensional results. Gothic gargoyles offset against a summer's rich blue sky can be stunning, while reflections in modern architecture create a maze of imagery. A night scene of a cathedral or church floodlit with tungsten light can make the building look heavenly while the same building shot under the light of the moon may look haunting.

One problem many architectural photographers come across is the effect the walls of tall buildings give of bending inwards towards the top of the picture. This is known as converging verticals and is made worse when a wide-angle lens is used from a low viewpoint. Some photographers will overemphasise this by getting really low to the ground and shooting on ultra-wide angles while others will do everything possible to avoid it. Professional architectural photographers will buy special equipment to correct the verticals.

Lenses for single-lens reflex cameras, known as shift lenses, can be used to make the walls parallel with the film plane by raising the front section of the lens parallel to the film plane. This can also be achieved using large-format cameras – a term known as rising front.

Sloping verticals can be corrected easily with the image-editing sotware's transform tool. In Photoshop you could use the perspective transformer.

Another way of avoiding converging verticals is to move much further away from the building and use a longer lens to fill the frame. If you move to a position where your viewpoint is roughly mid way up the building you'll avoid sloping walls altogether. To do this look for a hill, steps or office block where you may have access. You'll see some photographers carry a set of stepladders for the same reason, but that's a bit excessive.

Tips

Use an archway to frame another building, but watch the exposure. Move forward so that the arch cannot be seen and lock the exposure on the building that's the focal point. Then step back and take the shot with the framing archway in view.

Try using an archway or tree branch to frame a photograph.

If you can't get the whole building in view photograph it in several parts and join it together using stitching software in the computer.

Try taking a series of photographs of interesting features around a building and include pictures of the interior. Then turn them into a collage using the computer.

Don't worry anymore about scaffolding. You can remove this using the clone tool.

Watch out for items in the shot that could date the picture such as cars or people with clothing on that will go out of fashion.

Action

Whether it's the school's egg and spoon race, work's five-a-side football match, a visit to the grand prix or the hunting panther on the safari trip, capturing action provides one of the most challenging areas of photography. It's one of the most difficult subjects to master because you have to keep up with the moving subject while controlling the camera.

There are two ways to approach action. One is to ensure the photograph is as sharp as possible by freezing movement using a fast shutter speed. The other is to use a slower shutter speed and follow the subject as you press the shutter. This should blur the background while keeping the subject sharp. Using a fast shutter speed to freeze an acrobat mid-flight will look powerful, yet the same technique used on a rally car hurtling around the racetrack may make the car appear stationery.

The action mode ensures the camera selects a fast shutter speed to freeze movement.

If your camera doesn't have any manual shutter speed control you have to hope it's thinking on your wavelength. The odds are it won't be so we'll have to cheat on the computer. If, however, you do have control, try a few of these techniques. Set a slow shutter speed of around 1/15 of a second and pan with the subject, keeping your finger ready on the shutter release. As the subject approaches the point where you'd like to take the picture, press the shutter button fully down, but continue to follow the subject with the shutter depressed. If you perfect this technique the subject will be pin sharp and the background a blur, creating a dramatic sense of movement. Try it on running animals or cars and bikes.

Alternatively use the same shutter speed and keep the camera pointed at a point you know the moving subject will pass and take the picture as the subject comes into view. This will give a sharp background and a blurred subject, which can also look dramatic. This technique is great for subjects such as kids on swings, golfers swiping balls or abstract effects.

Pan with a moving subject to ensure it comes out sharp.

Close-ups

Most digital cameras have fantastic close-up ranges and filling the frame with flower heads, insects or collections is easy. As the lens is in a different position from the viewfinder you use to compose the picture you'll find the results are not accurate, unless the camera is a single-lens reflex where you look through the lens that takes the shot. If it has an LCD finder use this, otherwise you'll need to allow for the offset by framing up the shot manually.

Some cameras have a focusing system that moves automatically into the macro range as you become closer to the subject. If your model doesn't, make sure you've switched to the macro mode, usually indicated by a flower icon on the control panel.

Some cameras have such amazing close-focusing capabilities that they block light from part of the subject. Watch out for this and if it happens use a piece of white card to bounce light back into the shaded areas.

If your camera is disappointingly inadequate in the macro focusing arena, don't despair: you can buy supplementary close-up lenses

The camera's close-up mode is perfect for shooting insects, flowers and other similar sized objects.

for around £10 that fit in front of the camera lens. If the camera doesn't have a threaded lens you'll have to hold the close-up lens over it manually or buy an adaptor.

If you try to photograph the subject in extremely low light the flash will be activated and, depending on how close you are, the flash may be too far off to one side of the subject, resulting in an unevenly exposed picture. There are two ways around this: use a secondary slave flash to pump light into the scene – you can pick one up for about £10 – or make a small reflector out of card covered with silver foil and use this to bounce light back from the flash to illuminate the other side.

Tip

The depth of field at close range can be reduced so the front or back of the subject may appear soft. To ensure maximum sharpness either select a small aperture, or, if the camera doesn't have manual control, focus about $1/3$ of the way into the depth of the scene.

Night photography

One form of photography that's tricky to expose correctly is low light and night shots. The lighting easily fools the camera's light meter into either making the illumination overexposed or the overall scene too dark. The shutter speed is also long so your pictures will suffer from camera shake unless some form of support is used.

If the autoflash can be turned off, try resting the camera on something sturdy to take night scene modes using a slow shutter speed.

The support is the easy one to solve. Either use a tripod or brace yourself against a wall or fence.

With many digital cameras the exposure is not so easy. If it's an auto-only camera, first switch off the flash, which would otherwise activate. Then see if there's an exposure compensation feature, indicated with + and – symbols. These can be used to override the meter to help compensate for the dark surrounds. Try taking a picture first with the camera on auto and check the result on the LCD. Look at the shadow areas. Can you see any detail? If not, you need to overexpose to allow more light to fall on the CCD. Look at the highlights, streetlights, car headlights and windows. Are these overly bright without detail? If so, underexpose to prevent these washed out areas.

With this sort of photography the problem comes when the highlighted areas are burned out and the shadows are dense. You obviously can't under- and over-expose at the same time! The way round this digitally is to take two pictures, exposing one for the highlights and the other for the shadows, then merge the two in your image-editing package.

5 | ALL ABOUT SCANNERS

You don't have to own, or even use, a digital camera to produce digital pictures. Photographs taken on conventional film-based cameras can be transformed using a scanner. A scanner uses a CCD that travels across the path of the photograph to convert it into digital data.

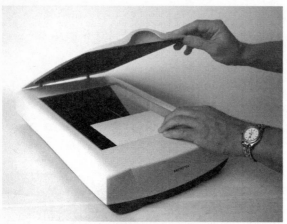

Flatbed scanner in use.

Various types of scanner are made, the most popular being the flatbed scanner. This looks like a miniature office photocopier and works in a similar way. Photographs or flat artwork are placed on the glass bed and the lid closes over to hold them against the glass. When the scanner is activated a fluorescent tube, positioned under the glass, tracks across the item to be copied. The light is reflected back through a series of mirrors and lenses to the CCD. The signals received by the CCD are then processed as a digital image.

Some flatbed scanners have the benefit of being able to replace the lid with a transparency hood. This positions the fluorescent tube above the glass scanning plate so slides, negatives and plates can be scanned on the same machine. While a transparency hood does increase versatility the quality is not always as good when images are blown up. A better option is to use a dedicated film scanner.

A film scanner has a slot to accept either individually mounted slides or strips of negatives or slides in a special carrier. The scanner works using a similar process to the flatbed models, but the resolution is much higher to ensure adequate magnification. The price of 35 mm film scanners has fallen dramatically and a decent model can now be picked up for around £250. A pro spec model that copes with medium- and large-format material will set you back over £3,000.

Film scanner in use.

One other type of scanner that you may come across is the drum scanner. Costing thousands of pounds, this is a high-end product used by repro houses to ensure the best results for magazines and book publishers. The material to be scanned is attached to a drum that rotates when scanning. Many repro houses offer a scanning service so you can benefit from drum scan quality without having to invest in one.

The specifications of a scanner determine how good it will be at converting your traditional photo into digital data. To do this there are three distinct areas – resolution, colour depth and dynamic range. The resolution is how many dots per inch the scanner captures, colour depth indicates how many colours it can see and dynamic range is the detail it can capture from shadows to highlights. We'll now look at each feature in more detail.

Resolution

Scanner manufacturers often quote two figures, for example 300×600 dpi. The first is the dots per inch that a scanner will record as the CCD travels across the width of the photo. This is the true optical resolution of the scanner and is the figure you should consider first. The second figure is the number of dots per inch that it can produce travelling down the length of the photo. If you choose the second figure in the scanner's properties window as the resolution the scanner will add the necessary number of dots to the first figure to ensure you end up with an image made up of 600 dpi. Adding these dots is a process known as interpolation. If you pick the first figure the scanner will produce a 300 dpi image discarding 300 pixels from the length.

Another figure that's often quoted is maximum resolution which is often as high as 9600 dpi. This is also an interpolated figure and should be avoided where possible. Having such high interpolation is often unnecessary anyway.

Colour depth

The scanner will have a figure quoted on its specification sheet of, say, 24-bit colour depth which means it's capable of creating any number of colours from a choice of 16.7 million. The benefit is that the image will appear more realistic than an 8-bit machine that will only record 256 colours. The latest scanners are capable of 36-bit colour depth that can produce billions of colours. This level of colour depth is remarkably true to life, but in many cases you'd be pushed to see a difference between images created using 24-bit and 36-bit colour depth.

Dynamic range

This is one of those figures that's often not quoted, but makers of the better quality models will include it on their specification sheets. It's basically an indication of how much shadow and highlight detail the scanner can record in one go. The shadow area of a film is known as the Dmax and the highlight area is the Dmin. The difference between the two figures is known as the density range and it's the scanner's job to capture as much of this as it can using its dynamic range. A higher figure will ensure that more detail is recorded.

A shot like this, taken in bright sunlight, will push a film to its limits, and a scanner will have an equally difficult job ensuring the highlight and shadow detail is captured.

The best models are around 4.2D and basic ones start at around 2.0D while most other scanners have a range of around 3.0D. These values are meaningless unless you have some idea of what a traditional film or print holds. The Dmax of a transparency film is around 3.3D and the Dmin is around 0.3D giving a dynamic range of 3.0D. Colour prints have a smaller range of around 2.0D and black & white photographs can be a little wider. If the scanner you buy has a dynamic range less than that of the medium that you're scanning you won't capture the full extent of tones. Basically, the higher the better. Having the extra detail recorded is recommended, even if you don't need it just yet.

Connecting to computer

A scanner can be connected to a computer in a variety of ways. Basic models plug into the computer's printer port. This is achieved in one of two ways. Either the manufacturer provides an adapter that connects into the back of the computer with a spare plug for the printer, or they are connected in a chain. More advanced models have a SCSI connection which gives a faster performance. Newer models have a USB connectivity that is the easiest to work with.

When the scanner is connected you have a simple installation procedure to run through using the scanner manufacturer's installation software wizard. This will ensure that the scanner is recognised by the computer when you're ready to start using it. Some models have a 'go' button on the front that activates the scanning software on the computer when you press it. Others are activated from within the scanning software, or from the Twain acquire source from your image-editing or optical character recognition (OCR) software.

How to get the best results

Despite what many people think, scanning is not as complicated as it seems. The big hang-up is resolution and the confusion is that scanning resolution never seems to match the quoted print resolution. Get the hang of how the figures correlate and you've cracked this black art.

Working out the resolution to scan at is easy. All you need to consider is what the output is going to be, then work backwards to calculate the necessary resolution. Let's say you want to make a photo on an inkjet printer that has a suggested output resolution of 200 dpi. So 200 dpi is the amount of dots you need to end up with. Any more will be wasted, any fewer and the quality won't be as good, because the printer doesn't have enough information to know what to do with the missing dots.

To work back you then look at the input medium. In this example, we'll have a 35 mm negative which is 1.5 inches in length. If you scanned this at 200 dpi you'd create a file that's 300 pixels in length (200 × 1.5). When you come to print the result it would appear the same size on paper, but what if, more likely, you want a 10 × 8 inch print? At 200 dpi you need a file with 2000 pixels (200 × 10). If you now go back to the scanner, set 1333 dpi on the software interface and click on the scan button you'll create your 2000 pixel image (1333 × 1.5).

Another way to calculate the resolution is divide the output length by the input length (in this example 10 ÷ 1.5 = 6.66) Then multiply the resulting figure with the printer's resolution (6.66 × 200 = 1333).

The same principle applies to scanning in prints. A popular sized 4 × 6 inch photo should be scanned in at 333 dpi if you want to make a 10 × 8 inch print on your 200 dpi printer. (Output length ÷ input length: 10 ÷ 6 = 1.66) (magnification increase × resolution: 1.66 × 200 = 333.)

Table 5.1 includes various input sizes along with output size and resolution.

Required output	Photograph to be scanned		
	4″ × 6″ print	10″ × 8″ print	35 mm slide
72 dpi 4″ × 6″ screen view	72 dpi	43 dpi	288 dpi
72 dpi A4 screen view	140 dpi	84 dpi	562 dpi
200 dpi inkjet print 4″ × 6″	200 dpi	120 dpi	800 dpi
200 dpi inkjet print A4	390 dpi	234 dpi	1560 dpi
200 dpi inkjet print A3	553 dpi	332 dpi	2212 dpi
300 dpi magazine repro 4″ × 6″	300 dpi	180 dpi	1200 dpi
300 dpi magazine repro A4	585 dpi	350 dpi	2340 dpi
300 dpi magazine repro A3	830 dpi	498 dpi	3318 dpi

Table 5.1 Optimum scanning resolution.

Once you've cracked resolution you should consider adjusting a few of the controls to ensure a sharper and punchier result. Most scanners will perform the scan, automatically adjusting colour balance, exposure, sharpness and density, but, like all autofunctions, there's room for error. Many of the problems encountered can be sorted out in the image-editing software, but it's better if you can cut out most of the work at the scanning stage.

Programs such as ScanWizard, that comes free with Microtek scanners, usually have very easy-to-follow interfaces with a choice of auto or plenty of manual control.

The first stage is to make a preview. This is a fast scanning method that lets you see a low-resolution preview of the final scan. From here you can crop to ensure you scan in just what you need and adjust controls to create a better final scan. Adjustments may include brightness and contrast; colour balance control to remove or introduce a colour cast; shadows and highlights to reposition the dark and lightest points in the scan; curves for more advanced contrast and brightness control and filters which includes the useful unsharp mask option. There's also a de-screen option to select the type of material that you're scanning from and prevent Moiré patterns appearing when scanning from magazines or newspapers.

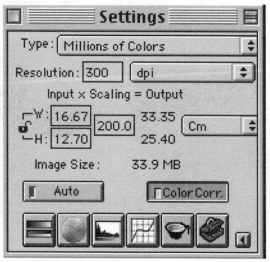

ScanWizard's interface is very easy to use. You can change the percentage increase and colour depth, but also click off auto and adjust everything manually.

The software will often give a before and after preview so you can see the effect the controls are having on the image. The preview picture is usually too small to see clearly what's going on, but it's better than nothing.

When you're happy with the level of adjustment click on final to create a scan that includes all your settings. It's worth spending a little time with the manual areas to perfect a few adjustments to produce better scans. The adjustments can be saved and applied to future images and you should end up with a number of settings that can be applied on specific jobs.

Tips

Always keep the glass surface of your flatbed scanner clean. Use a soft cloth and some cleaning fluid that you'd use for the computer monitor.

If your program doesn't recognise the scanner make sure that the Twain driver is in the correct plug-in or Twain folder and reboot the computer.

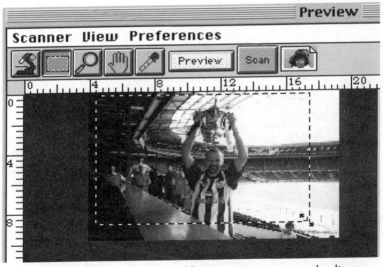

The preview image appears quickly so you can crop and adjust before making the full scan.

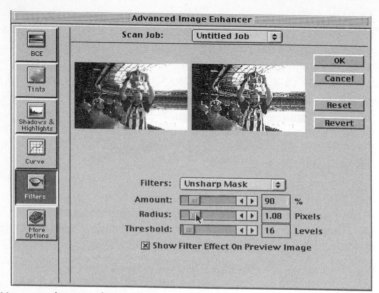

You can sharpen the picture using the unsharp mask mode so it comes out better when scanned.

Try scanning in shallow three-dimensional objects such as shells, buttons and coins.

Try placing a 3D object on the scanner, but take care not to scratch the glass.

Alternative to a scanner

If you have a digital camera and a range of traditional pictures you'd like converting to digital you could consider an alternative to a film scanner. Some digital cameras have a filter thread to which you could attach a slide copier to use the camera to convert your pictures digitally. This saves you buying a scanner, but results depend, obviously, on the optical quality and resolution of the camera.

6 | OTHER WAYS TO FIND DIGITAL PICTURES

You don't have to own a scanner or a digital camera to produce digital images. If you have a collection of pictures or still prefer to shoot on a film based camera and can't justify a high quality scanner; you have the option of using a processing lab or bureau to scan in your negatives or transparencies. The lab uses a high-end machine and then outputs the images onto a storage medium for you to take away and use at home.

Labs have been offering a variety of services for a number of years now, but Kodak was the first to realise this was a useful option and developed the PhotoCD in 1994. Unfortunately, at that time, Kodak were a little too far ahead of the game and the system didn't generate the mass market needed to advertise and promote the system to its full potential.

The system provided a multi-level resolution set of pictures, comprising five folders, each at different resolutions, containing the same range of pictures. The idea was that you could select and work on the image at the resolution required: screen size for cataloguing, two slightly higher resolutions for use on the Internet and in computer editing, a size to print out a 4 × 6 inch picture and one for A4.

While the system had its advantages many of the software manufacturers didn't develop their programs to accept the .pcd format used for the images, so it was quite confusing.

Now things are different and Kodak has returned with the more appropriate Picture CD service. Instead of the .pcd format Kodak has adopted the universally accepted JPEG format and made the system far more user-friendly.

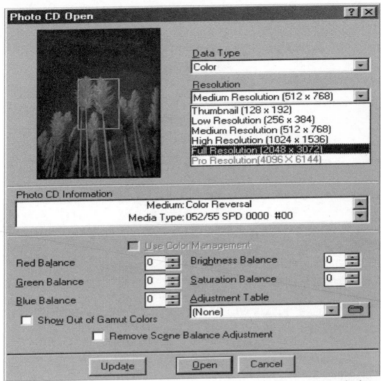

When you try and open a PhotoCD image you're greeted with this screen that lets you choose the size of image you open along with a range of corrections you could make.

If you hand a film in at your local processor you now have the option of ticking a box that instructs the lab to digitize your pictures and another box indicates whether you want the pictures returned on a floppy disk or Picture CD. The floppy disk provides screen resolution images that you can print out at small sizes.

The Picture CD is a much better option. Here the images are provided within a magazine-style interface. As you load the CD a cover appears and clicking on this takes you into the contents page where you have the choice of looking at your pictures, editing them, trying out free software and printing pictures. It's all intuitive stuff and you'll soon be adding captions, enhancing and printing your digital images.

All your pictures appear as thumbnail images.

Clicking on a picture opens it and offers various editing controls.

Download from Web/royalty-free disk

You don't even have to own a camera to create digital images. There are many sources from which you can obtain pictures to use in your own creations. You may have an idea in your mind and with a little searching you'll find all the images you need.

One source of free pictures is royalty-free CDs. These often contain images and clip art that can be used freely for your own creations. Royalty-free CDs can be bought from most software suppliers and you'll often find samplers with a limited number of pictures supplied as cover mounts on the front of magazines.

Companies such as PhotoDisc, IMSI and Corel have a vast range of CDs to choose from. PhotoDisc tends to categorize their product so you could buy a CD comprising 100 high resolution images containing, for example, patterns, people or animals, whereas IMSI prefer the pack-it-all-in approach and its CDs contain everything from pictures of animals to decorative designs to road signs. The PhotoDisc approach is useful if you're after a cover for a CD, book or brochure.

IMSI packages often include a couple of dozen CDs and a book the size of a telephone directory showing tiny thumbnails of all the hundreds of thousands supplied. Fortunately, they also include a useful search program that pinpoints your specific need. Type in 'moose' and pictures, graphics, typefaces and anything else connected with 'moose', for instance, will appear in a library from where you can select and open the image you want to work with. The size of these files is usually quite small but the images are great as additions to newsletters, illustrations, stationary or for inclusion as part of an overall image.

You don't have to buy a collection of CDs if you're connected to the Internet. You could key in the words 'picture of the moon' and the browser would go off and search for pictures of the moon. Then, depending on the sites the browser finds, you could download for free, or for an indicated repro charge, a picture of the moon. Royalty-free pictures often have conditions of use. Read these carefully before using the picture. Images can often only be used for personal projects so anything that is seen as profit making would prevent their use.

Many sites are now set up to sell you pictures for a variety of uses. Once again Corel and PhotoDisc are big in this arena, but the traditional picture libraries such as Tony Stone and Images also offer image purchasing over the Internet. Here you're free to search through their vast libraries using keywords and when you find the image you want you have the option of purchasing a digital copy for use.

The cost depends on what you intend doing with the picture. If it's going on the front of a staff report that goes to a dozen or so employees the royalty fee will be much less than a picture that's going to be used on a record cover that may be seen by millions of people.

Like shopping for groceries you can go around the site collecting images in a basket or cart and then go to the checkout to add up the bill. You then pay the fee using a credit card and download the pictures. This can take up a fair amount of time on your phone as each image will transfer at the rate of your modem.

Using my previous example of the moon I keyed into the browser lunar pictures which brought up a list of suggested locations to visit, including: **http://www.sunlink.net/~torff/lunar.html** – this site has a great selection of moon images, but, as with many sites, the pictures may not be used without permission. The benefit of e-mail is that you can contact the Web site owner with ease. Another site that I already knew about didn't appear in the search, but keying in the word NASA brought me to it: **http://www.nasa.gov/gallery** has a massive archive of over 500,000 images, including ones of the moon. The pictures can be used freely so it's a great resource.

When you find a picture you'd like to use click the right button on the PC's mouse and select the save to disk option. Choose a location and the downloading begins. On a Mac just grab the picture and drag it to the desktop.

Downloading pictures can be costly so check the picture's file size before you attempt this to give an indication of how long it will take. A 1084 × 1025 pixel file took me two and a half minutes to download using a home 56 KB modem. The PC has a useful size/download speed/download time indicator but it's not all that accurate – according to it my example download should have taken over three minutes.

You'll also notice other options on the right mouse menu including saving the downloaded image as a screen saver or desktop pattern.

One of the best sites for free pictures is UK based Freefoto at: **http://www.freefoto.com**. With 21 main sections and 299 subheadings you'll find over 5000 images and they're free, providing you only download them for private use. You can also buy the pictures if they're going to be used for commercial purposes.

7 | IMAGE MANIPULATION

The camera never lies

This is a powerful statement, and one that has had its fair share of coverage in the media, creating wide and heated debates over the years. It's quite easy to see arguments for and against the statement and either way would be valid. One thing's for sure, though, with the aid of digital photography the camera can lie, lie and lie again.

Painters have always been able to bend the truth, whether adding moody lighting to a dull sky, removing wrinkles from the ageing person whose portrait they're painting, or taking out the ugly distractions in a scene. Photography made it possible for ordinary folk with less skill than an artist to capture the memories, but unless they were competent in darkroom skills they would have to make do with a picture that recorded the truth – warts and all. Digital photography is akin to painting. With the aid of a computer you can perform magic that had previously been a black art in photography and a skill for the talented painter.

Digital image makers can do everything the painter could do to cheat, but they can also add realism that only a photographer can do with ease. With the right bit of software you can create amazing images from the heart and mind. The approach you take to digital imaging depends on your artistic capabilities. As editor of the UK's leading digital-imaging magazine I have seen thousands of creations submitted by readers from around the world. The variety is stunning. Ranging from images that you'd stake your life savings on that they aren't digital to works of art that have never seen a photograph. I have an open mind on the subject. You may suggest I am sitting on the fence, but I wouldn't like to push digital imaging down a particular road. As far as I'm concerned everything goes – be creative, be expressive, be yourself, and, most of all, have fun.

Digital PhotoFX is the UK's leading digital-imaging magazine and features the work of many digital artists each issue. Some pictures are subtle enhancements, some are creative alterations, others are fantasies.

In this unit we'll take a look at the types of software available for all sorts of applications, including image manipulation, graphic work, design, Web creation, 3D and morphing. We will look at various interfaces and include a back-to-basics guide to how you load up and use programs. We'll also highlight some must-have programs to kick-start your image making activities.

Retouching programs

The most popular program for digital image makers is retouching software, also referred to as image-editing, image-manipulation or image-enhancing software. This type of product has a variety of tools to shift pixels around, change their colour, duplicate them, remove them, add effects and much more. It's used to make your digital pictures much better whether as a simple enhancement, as a major renovation or as part of a project such as a greetings card or poster.

Photoshop

Now over 10 years old the industry standard in this category is Adobe Photoshop. Originally developed by Lucas for the movie industry it started to be adopted by professional graphic houses in the early 1990s and soon photographers caught on to its superb flexibility. Now sold as version 6.0 many changes and improvements have been made to make it the leader in the enthusiast market. There are over 60,000 registered users in the UK and no doubt thousands more running illegal copies.

Photoshop has a vast range of facilities to take your images from base to output. The program supports dozens of file formats and can optimise images for use on the Web using Adobe Image Ready. The huge range of filters supplied to apply soft focus, artistic effects, lighting, textures and much more can be supplemented with optional third party plug-in programs that run seamlessly from within the Photoshop interface. Many are free and can be down-loaded from the manufacturers' Web sites.

Picture Publisher

Photographers will benefit from the range of exposure tools that use familiar language such as lens flare, lighting and depth of field effects. Like Photoshop it has a vast range of features, but isn't considered seriously by the graphics world. For the home user it's a powerful package with lots to offer.

MGI PhotoSuite

PhotoSuite continues to be the leading program in the budget market. The interface is very user-friendly with balloon messages appearing as you run the cursor over on-screen buttons and graphics. The step by step approach makes it simple for inexperienced users to get to grips with scanning, editing, printing and e-mailing pictures. The latest version comes with a picture-stitching feature and a mosaic/tapestry making option. It's extremely versatile, but less advanced than some.

Photo Soap

Many features are hidden by the unconventional interface. Tools such as brushes and erasers look the part while storage drawers pop in and out as required. If you're used to normal program interfaces this one offers novelty value, but it may get in the way as you work. One that needs to be tried before you buy.

Corel Photo-Paint

Corel packages Photo-Paint as a bundle with a drawing program. It's a powerful program that offers a similar interface to Photoshop so you have to have a rough idea of how to work your way around this to benefit from the huge range of feature options. This is a program that's also considered in the graphics world and now that it's also available in Mac format it's a serious threat to Photoshop. Like Photoshop, most third party plug-ins will work with it.

PhotoDeluxe

Some would call this Photoshop junior. Now in version 4 it takes many of the Photoshop retouching features and filters, adds a series of stationery templates and hides the power behind a step by step format. Clicking on 'get picture' gives you access to the scanner or camera software and each stage from there on is managed with ease.

Photo Impact

Another program that has developed from being a me-too product to a more adventurous item. The latest version has loads of useful stuff to help you create great images and lots of graphics for Web-based projects. It's also decent on the text and frame creations.

Paint Shop Pro

A program that has more users than any other simply because it's been given away as trials on the Internet for years. Now in version 6 it offers all the power of Photoshop with lots of extras, for at least a quarter of the price. All the layer features and blending modes are included along with a useful Picture Tubes feature that lets you repeat patterns around the image by painting objects using the paint brush. If you have £100 to spend this is the program to buy – it's stunning.

The program also comes with Animation Shop that helps you create animated GIFs for use on Web sites and presentations.

Paint programs

Paint programs can be used to make digital paintings from scratch or add a touch of artistic flare to a digital photograph.

Painter

Painter is an amazing program that can be used alongside Photoshop to increase its versatility. The package comes in a real paint tin and has a colourful manual to help you through the program. A wide variety of brushes can be used to paint in charcoal, oils, watercolours and more and when the paints are overlaid they react in a similar way to real ones making the effects outstanding. There are a number of pre-set painting styles such as Van Gogh that can also be applied to a photo.

Deep Paint

Developed by a New Zealand company, Deep Paint can be used as a plug-in with Photoshop or independently. It works by painting watercolour, oil, felt pen, pencil or chalk onto a new layer above the original. The brush clones colour and detail from the lower layer and applies the chosen paint style onto the new layer. The base layer is reduced in opacity so you mostly see the effect of the brush. It's less versatile than Painter, but may be a worthwhile choice if you only want to convert your photos into paintings.

Design programs

These programs are used by all design bureaux and publishers who create documents, books, magazines and catalogues using the software to position pictures, add and format text and set into a neat page ready for printing.

QuarkXPress

This is the industry standard and is now in version 4.1. Picture and text boxes can be arranged with precision. There's a Bézier curve drawing tool allowing text to wrap more freely around objects.

Shortcut commands are logical and there are many third-party plug-ins to increase its versatility. With add-ons such as Extensis' Beyond Press you can convert the page to HTML for use on the Web.

Serif Page Plus

An entry-level design program that has a number of templates to help you produce your own business stationery and greetings card etc. It allows you to call up a template and edit, replacing text, adding graphics, resizing and repositioning elements within the layout. Use these first to become familiar with how the program works then move on and do your own thing.

Adobe Indesign

Adobe are making an attempt to eat into QuarkXPress' territory. In the graphics industry XPress and Photoshop are the leading two programs so it makes sense for Adobe to have a slice of the design area. By making Indesign run seamlessly with Photoshop it creates a unique package for the publisher. It may have several advantages over XPress, but not the history.

PageMaker

Until recently PageMaker had a similar coverage in design bureaux as XPress, but as Quark has improved PageMaker has lost some ground. PageMaker has the advantage of being able to split palettes making it better for customising your working space and it supports Twain drivers which means that you can access pictures direct from the scanner or digital camera. It also comes with a table editor that is an optional extra for XPress.

Web creation

As Internet service providers (ISPs) continue to offer free accounts with loads of Web space thrown in, one of the hottest programs currently is the Web site creation software. This program overcomes the difficulty of having to learn HyperText Markup

Language (HTML) that's used to create a page and does all the hard work for you, leaving the HTML code hidden in the background.

Go Live

Now owned by Adobe to complete its range of professional specified design and image editing software.

Pages can be laid out using guides and rules for accurate positioning and a colour picker ensures the colour you choose will be Web safe. If you understand the language you can view the page as it has been written in HTML.

Dreamweaver

Powerful authoring program from Macromedia that uses WYSIWYG HTML editing. Parts of this code can then be protected from editing while other areas remain editable. You can also add pictures, text and graphics in layers and then convert them into tables making them compatible with most browsers.

Front Page

A basic program that's also provided as a limited version free with Windows PCs. Coming from Microsoft it works seamlessly with other programs from the Office Suite. Fifty templates are provided to help you produce your first site and the WYSIWYG frames editing feature makes it easy to lay out and manage objects within the pages.

Pagemill

Adobe's alternative to Front Page lets you easily organize frames and tables to pages. You can type in words, reformat, change the colour and add pictures or graphics with ease. Spreadsheets can also be imported directly from Microsoft Excel and Internet Explorer is provided so you can see how the site is shaping up.

3D

If the thought of creating objects with depth appeals, consider one of these 3D programs that provide opportunities to create stunning landscapes in either natural or sci-fi styles. By stretching and adding to a wire frame you build up a terrain that can then be filled with surface texture, lit from any angle, adding haze or fog and a background sky. The terrain can be rotated through 360° to see how it looks from all angles.

Bryce

The most popular program by far in this field lets you create landscapes with stunning realism. Add a sun or moon to your creation and control the lighting, shadow intensity and position for amazing results. Although billed as a program for beginners as well as professional it's quite complex and the interface may appear daunting on your first view visits.

Vue d'Esprit

French program with similar terrain building to Bryce with a less elaborate interface, but still equally challenging to grasp early on. This package includes a Solid Growth Vegetation generator to add natural-looking trees to your landscapes. The back of the instruction manual includes a series of tutorials to help you get the most out of the program.

Morphing

Software such as Avid Elastic Reality takes one image and morphs it into another through several stages. The first image could be a picture of you and the second your mother or father. Key points are taken from around the facial features of both pictures to build a map of the faces and then the software begins to map out the positions as the face changes from one to the other. Interesting for a while, but you could soon get fed up of it.

Using the programs

Now you've seen the range of software you'll no doubt be itching to get going and use some. The first stage is to load the software onto your computer. All the latest programs come with easy install options. You load the CD into the drive and an installation start-up screen usually appears. If not, you should locate the CD drive and click on the window to open up the contents and locate the set-up folder on a PC or the installation icon on the Mac. Clicking on these will call up the set up window. Here you're given the option to read the software licence and agree to accept it. The set-up ends if you don't accept. The agreement basically asks you not to copy or use the program illegally. Click accept and the load options appears.

You now usually have the option of performing a custom install or loading the recommended items. Sometimes a program may include a file that's already included on your computer. Then a message will appear saying the current version is older or newer than the one you intend loading and asks if you want to replace it or keep the existing file. Choose the latest version.

The installer will also ask where you want the program to be saved. Creating a folder for programs to keep them all together makes it easier to locate later. Once installed the program's icon will appear at the selected destination and can be double-clicked to run the program. At some stage you will be asked for a serial number. It's usually a long number comprising letters and numbers and needs careful keying in. The program won't run without it.

Now you're ready to turn to the next unit to see what key features image-editing programs have.

8 | ESSENTIAL TOOLS

All image-editing programs have a selection of tools you can use to perform certain tasks when applied to a picture. The main ingredients of the toolbox are explained here so you know what to look for when you're choosing a suitable program.

Selection tools

These are vital and all programs have some form of selection tools. They're split into five types: marquee, lasso, pen tool, magic wand and masks. The tool's job is to select an object, or area, within a photograph so it can be copied and pasted into another area or image, or worked on by applying colour effects or filters without affecting its surroundings. An active selection will have a border of thin dotted lines known as a marquee or, to some, marching ants.

Marquee tools

The marquee tools are adjustable frames that can be pulled over a photograph to select a rectangular area or an ellipse within the image. You can usually hold down the shift key to ensure the marquee stays square or circular when you draw or increase its size. Some programs have a preference to set the marquee up to a fixed size or fixed ratio. This is useful if you're copying images from one location to another and need the copied piece at a certain size. Use them when you want to select an object that's the same shape as the marquee or to select a lump of background to cover up another area.

Drag the rectangular or circular marquee over the area you want to cut out or select.

Lasso

The lasso tool is more useful when the object isn't regular. As the name implies drawing with this tool places a lasso marquee around the subject. Use it by magnifying the image and working carefully around the subject that you want to select. The basic freehand lasso goes where the cursor goes in as irregular path as you like. It's useful for selecting round complicated areas to make the cut out, but a steady hand is needed. You can usually add to the selected area by holding down the shift key as you draw, or take away from the selection by holding down the alt (PC) or option (Mac) key.

The polygon lasso is better when the object has straight edges because it adds a straight line between clicks making it easier to draw around less complex subjects.

Another lasso that's recently appeared within Photoshop and is found in some other programs is a magnetic lasso. This one latches

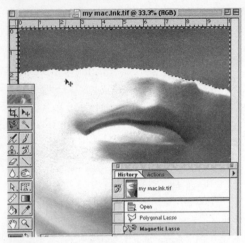

Draw around the edge of the subject using the freehand or magnetic lasso to make a selection.

on to edge detail and can be used quite quickly, providing the tolerance value is set to suit the image.

Pen tool

This is a more complicated selection tool that offers fantastic control once you get used to it. The pen tool allows Bézier curves to be created, making it easy to select smooth curved areas and shapes. A selection made with the pen tool also has the option of being saved as a clipping path for import into QuarkXPress. The clipping path tells the program that there's no background and will allow text to run around the cut out picture.

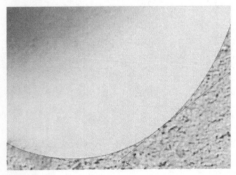

The pen tool should be used when you want an accurate selection of a curved subject.

Magic wand

This is by far the easiest selection tool providing the area to be selected is of similar tone but different from the unwanted area. It works by selecting all pixels within a pre-selected tolerance range. By clicking on a sample area it picks all other pixels with similar values. It's often the background that is more appropriate to select using this tool; then you'd use the inverse selection option to switch from the background to the required subject. Once again, if the selection isn't accurate you can revert to a lasso and use the shift and alt/option keys to add or take away any untidy bits.

The magic wand selects all the pixels within a similar value, so it's useful for subjects like this with an uncomplicated background.

Masks

Masks form a great visual way of seeing which area is selected. The mask can then be turned into a selection. Masks are painted on using greyscale and a paintbrush. White adds more mask while black erases it. The area that's being painted will have a colour – usually red – and you can magnify the image and paint red into the smallest and most complicated areas.

Some programs, such as Photoshop, also have a colour range option that selects all pixels with a certain pre-selected colour range. The benefit of this is being able to pick larger objects with ease. Say you want to turn a green apple red, you'd point the eye-dropper at the apple and click. A fuzziness slider adjusts the range of greens the eye-dropper picks so you can adjust until the whole apple appears selected.

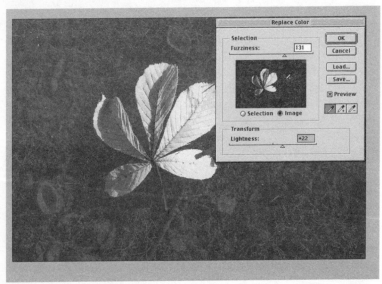

Using a mask makes it easier to see what is and isn't selected. This selection can be increased and decreased using the rubber and paintbrush tools.

Crop tool

This is the first tool you should use to crop your digital picture, removing any unwanted edge detail which all adds to the file size of the image. You click in one corner and drag down diagonally to the opposite corner to create a frame. Then when you click in the middle of the frame all the pixels on the outside are removed and the picture's file size is reduced accordingly.

Use the crop tool to remove unwanted pixels from around the edge of the picture.

Layers

Layers are essential if you intend creating complex images. Layers, called objects in some programs, are like sheets of glass placed on top of one another, each layer holding parts of the image. The stacked layers make the overall image and each can be moved in position up or down the stack and edited individually. Individual layers can also be turned off so you can see what effect they're having on the overall image.

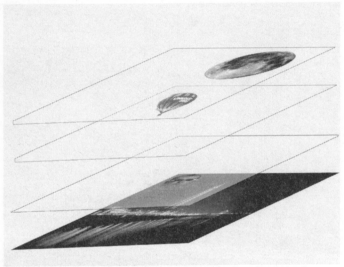

Layers are like sheets of acetate on top of one another, each containing part of the image.

Using layers makes it possible to apply effects without messing up the whole picture. Just copy a layer that you want to change and switch the original layer off.

Layers can be used to hold text, backgrounds and image content. Features, such as Photoshop's adjustment layers, mean you can do things to the overall picture and turn the layer off if you don't want the effect to print out or be viewed. (See colour plates 8 & 9.)

Clone tool,

If there's one tool that reinforces the benefits of digital photography it's the clone tool, or rubber stamp. You only have to see this in action to be in awe at the power. It works by sampling pixels from one area and dropping them down in another. You first select the area you want to sample from by placing the cursor over it and click on the mouse. Then move to the area you want the pixels to be placed and click and drag to paint in replicated pixels.

The clone tool can be used to duplicate detail in one picture or, as in the case of this moon, to copy from one image to another.

Two options are usually available – align and non-align. Align ensures the sample point cursor follows the one that you're painting at the cloned source. Non-align picks up from the sample point that it was last at when the mouse was released.

The clone tool is a favourite for image restorers who sample bits from other areas of the picture to repair scratched and torn photos. It's also ideal for removing spots and blemishes, telegraph poles from scenic shots, people you don't want in group photos and much more.

Eraser

The eraser is a basic tool that removes detail from the image, replacing it with the background colour. The new Magic Eraser on Photoshop 5.5 replaces the background with a transparency and is useful for making cut outs.

The top part has been erased using the normal eraser that replaces the subject with the background colour. The bottom half has been erased using Photoshop's Magic Eraser, which replaces the subject with a transparent background.

Painting tools

Paintbrushes

These are used to add colour to selected parts of the image or to paint a picture from scratch. There are various types and most can be edited. The normal shape is round and its size can be varied from single pixel coverage to hundreds of pixels, although bigger ones can make the painting strokes sluggish and are less accurate.

The paintbrush can be changed in size and shape in most programs.

You also have the option to feather the edge of the brush to soften the paint stroke. In some programs there's a wet edge stroke that gives the paint a watercolour feel. Changing the shape of the brush is useful if you want to apply elliptical strokes. This gives the effect of a calligraphy pen. There's also a range of custom brushes usually offered. In Photoshop 5.5 these are found in the Goodies folder. On a PC, using Paint Shop Pro you have the choice of the Picture Tubes mode that samples a graphic or area of an image and repeats it as you paint.

Airbrush

An alternative to the paintbrush is an airbrush. This lays paint down at a selected pressure and the softer this is the more control you have on the result. Paint can be built up so start with a very low opacity and build up to the desired colour. If you want a straight line click the starting point on the picture then hold down the shift key, reposition the mouse and click again.

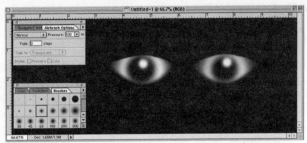

The airbrush is best used for graphic or artist applications.

Programs such as Paint Shop Pro and Photoshop have several blending modes that allow the painted pixels to react in a different way with the existing ones.

Pencil tool

Works like the paintbrush, but draws a hard-edged line so the results will probably have jagged edges.

Smudge tool

The smudge tool with an icon of a pointing finger blurs pixels by pushing them in a chosen direction. This is a useful option when you want to soften areas such as blemishes on someone's face or to extend hair around cut outs to make the result look less jagged and the hair appear more realistic. Some digital photographers go over the whole picture randomly smudging areas to make the image take on a dreamy appearance.

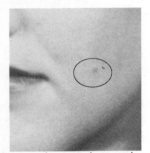 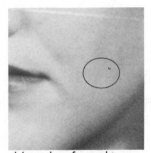

The smudge can be used to remove blemishes from skin.
Left: Before. Right: After.

Dodge and burn tools

Named after the popular darkroom techniques, dodge and burn tools have the same effect. The dodge tool dodges the pixels below it making the image appear to receive less exposure so it becomes lighter. The burn tool has the opposite effect and increases the exposure in the underlying area, resulting in the pixels being darkened. You can usually adjust the exposure and it's better to have a low exposure and gradually build up the effect by going over the same area again.

Dodge and burn tools shown here lightening and darkening part of this boat. The dodge tool has made the wood white while the burn tool has increased the shadow density to make it rich black.

Magnifier

The magnifier or zoom tool is used to make the image bigger on screen. You can usually increase the magnification to 1600% and focus in on individual pixels. Use this at high magnifications for accurate editing and pull back to check the results. The ideal magnification to work at depends on the job in hand and can be a case of trial and error.

Use the zoom tool or magnifier to increase the number of pixels to make it easier to edit fine detail and check for accuracy.

Paint bucket

The paint bucket, also known as a fill or flood fill tool in some programs, fills a selection with the currently selected colour. It's quicker to use this than painting in the selection using a large brush.

The paint bucket drops the chosen colour onto pixels with similar value.

Gradient tool

This fills the canvas with a graduated colour from the foreground to background colour. It can also be used as a layer mask to blend two pictures together. Set the layer up so the mask goes from foreground to transparent and the upper layer shows through where the mask is clear and the base layer where the foreground colour blocks it. The gradient of the mask ensures the result blends smoothly. This is a great tool for blending complex images when making montages.

The gradient tool will produce a graduated effect from the foreground to background colour.

Image Sprayer

A tool that comes with Corel's Photo-Paint that is used to spray an image across the picture, similar to the Picture Tubes mode in Paint Shop Pro. It's perfect for adding extra flowers to a garden or clouds in the sky.

The Image Sprayer in Photo-Paint or Picture Tubes in Paint Shop Pro can be used to paint repetitive images across a picture. Here grass, flies, snails, leaves and fire were added to illustrate the feature.

Object transparency tool

Another item found in Corel's Photo-Paint that lets you fade areas of the object so it begins to blend with the background.

Corel's Object transparency tool helps blend two layers together.

Eye-dropper

The icon looks just like an eye-dropper and is used to sample a pixel colour by placing the tip over the one you require. This is useful if you want an exact colour match elsewhere in the picture. One area you may want to use this is where you decide to put a colour border around the picture. You can sample part of the image and use that colour to create the matching border.

The eye-dropper is used to sample the colour of pixels from part of the picture.

9 | SIMPLE ENHANCEMENTS

Image editing can be as complex and intricate as you'd like to make it but there are also plenty of simple techniques that can improve your family album.

Throughout this unit we'll look in detail at some of these basic techniques and take you through each process step by step.

Red-eye removal

One of the most common faults with family snaps taken with flash is red-eye effect. This is where the pupils of the subject's eyes take on a bright red glow. It's caused because the flash is too close to the camera's lens and the light hits the back of the eye, lighting up the blood vessels which makes the normally dark pupil red. Most cameras have a red-eye reduction mode that uses a method of preflash to make the pupil size reduce and lessen the effect of red-eye. Unfortunately, few are effective, and even the best only reduce the effect and don't eliminate it all together.

The way round this digitally is to select the area and change the colour, here's how.

Step 1 First magnify the eyes on screen so you have a large area to work on.

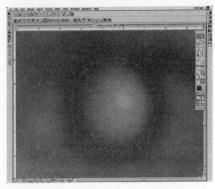

Step 2 Choose a method of selecting the red area. Select either the magic wand set to the right tolerance or use the elliptical marquee to draw a circle the size of the pupil, or draw around using the magnetic or freehand lasso. Set a feather of around 10 pixels to soften the edge.

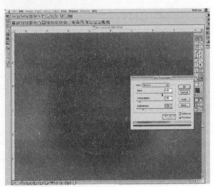

Step 3 Now you need to change the colour. Choose the hue and saturation command, Image> Adjust> Hue/Saturation (Photoshop). Change the hue to a yellow/ brown or blue, depending on the colour you want the pupil to have. Reduce the saturation to bring down the glow and adjust the lightness to make the colour dull.

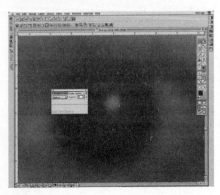

Step 4 Repeat Step 3 on the other eye and zoom back to check that the effect looks natural. If it does save the file, if not revert to the previous version and try again.

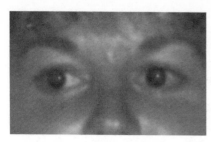

Step 5 Use the dodge tool set to a low opacity and go over the catchlight to make the area brighter. This will add sparkle to the eyes.

Do it with your eyes shut

Some programs have an auto red-eye removing mode that works by looking at the pixels in the selected area and changing their colour. The process works quite well, but can occasionally leave a few missed red pixels around the edges of the eye.

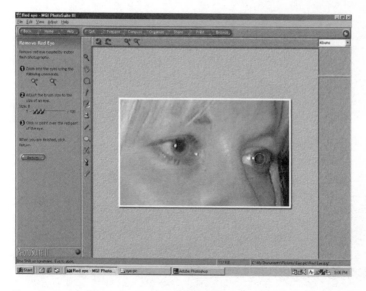

To remove red-eye using MGI Photo Suite you simply choose a brush roughly the same size as the pupil and paint to desaturate any red pixels that you brush over.

Feathering edges

Edges of a selection are hard so whatever you do to the selection, such as changing the colour, copying and pasting or apply a filter effect, will have a harsh edge. Applying a feather to the edge gradually reduces the opacity of the pixels at either side of the marching ants. Setting a larger number in the feather palette will increase the number of pixels either side of the selection. Doing this ensures that the edge becomes soft so the selection and any applied effect blends better with surrounding pixels.

The amount of feathering depends on the image size. A 640 × 480 pixel image, for example, will need less feathering than a 1600 × 1200 pixel image, as the pixels in the feather are proportional to the overall picture.

In the red-eye reduction technique, I used a feather of ten pixels. Any less and the result would have been a harshly coloured circle in the centre any more and the softness of the blend would have been too apparent.

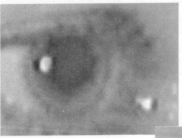
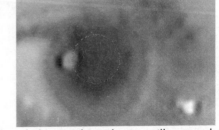

Left: If you select the pupil and change the colour you'll notice the result will be a harsh circle. Right: Feathering the selection to obtain a smoother circle

Colour change

Changing the colour of part of the picture is useful in many instances. Perhaps you'd like to see what a different colour hairstyle would look like. You could mess with nature and invent green roses – the ideas are endless.

Step 1 Select the object that's going to have the colour change. We thought this woman's red jacket could do with being less of a contrast to the yellow rape field. At the time of taking the picture it seemed fine, but a few years and fashions have passed since then!

Step 2 Selecting the jacket using the magic wand would normally be easy with this colour selection as all the red pixels are of similar tone and are not present elsewhere. The problem is that the yellow flowers cover a lot of the jacket and selecting in between is difficult. Programs can deal with complex selections like this, using a replace colour mode.

Step 3 Select the replace colour option and use the eye-dropper tool to sample an area of the jacket. Pixels within the similar red value will show up as white on the image in the colour range preview window. Adjusting the fuzziness slider adds pixels when you increase the value and takes away pixels when decreased. When you have as much of the item selected as required, click OK.

Step 4 The original image now has the marching ants selection but not all over the jacket. We still have to add to this using the magic wand or, if your program has it, the similar mode that picks up other pixels with similar values.

Step 5 Now the face is also selected so we remove this using the lasso tool with the alt key held down. Make a lasso selection around the face and remove the unwanted area of selection.

Step 6 Now use the hue and saturation command to change the colour of the selected red pixels. I thought blue was a suitable colour. You may think differently. (See colour plate 4.)

Adjusting contrast

When an image from a film is scanned into the computer it can sometimes lack contrast, resulting in flat lifeless tones. Black & white photographers using film-based cameras have always been able to expose and develop their films to maximize contrast. Variable contrast papers are available to darkroom users who want to vary results from their negatives.

With an image-editing program it's easy to improve badly processed pictures using the brightness/contrast mode. The mode looks at the range of pixels and adjusts the difference between the lightest and darkest points. A low contrast image has light and dark areas much closer to the mid-point resulting in a flat image and adjusting contrast to stretch these points boosts the highlight and shadow areas. A high-contrast image has a large gap between the darkest and lightest point, sometimes so much so that there are few tones in between. Reducing contrast brings these extremes closer to the mid point.

In this example a picture of a jug and dish were underexposed and underdeveloped, resulting in a flat black & white image. Call up the contrast control. In Photoshop that's, Image>Adjust>Brightness/Contrast. Then adjust the contrast slider until you're happy with the result. You may want to adjust the brightness at the same time and experiment with both controls to achieve the best overall balance.

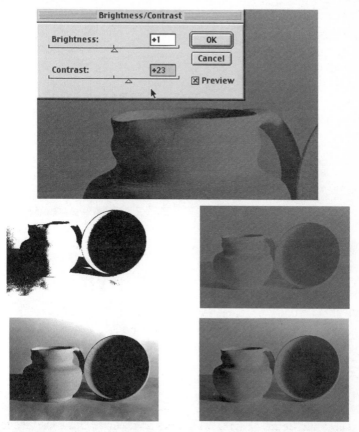

Step by step adjusting contrast. Adjust the contrast slider too far to the right and the picture becomes black and white with no mid-tones. Adjust the contrast slider too far to the left and the picture becomes dull grey with no black or white tones. A position somewhere in between gives the best result, although it is a matter of personal taste.

Hue

The hue control changes the colour of the selected pixels shifting the image colour. Use this if you want to change the whole feel of an image or make surreal pictures. (See colour plate 3.)

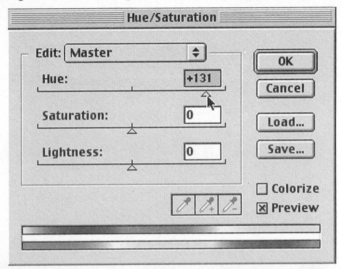

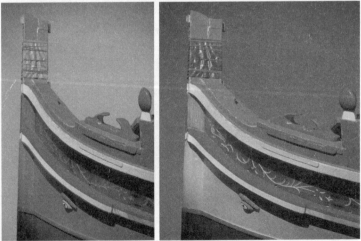

The hue control is used to change the colour of pixels. The two boat pictures show the effect of selecting different positions on the hue slider.

Saturation

Saturation controls the colour's strength. With setting from −100 to +100 you can remove all trace of colour, producing a monotone image or increase colours, making them unnaturally vibrant.

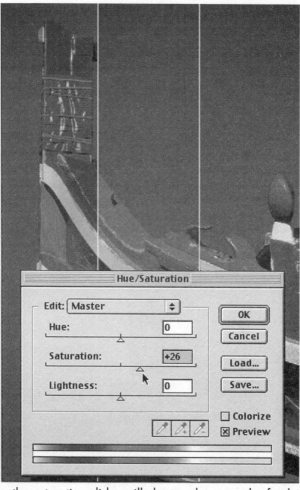

Adjusting the saturation slider will change the strength of colours in the picture. (See colour plate 4.)

Use this to make colours leap out of the picture by setting the slider to between +30 and +50 or give a subdued pastel look by setting around −50. Once again, you can adjust saturation for just part of the image maybe decreasing the value for a background to make the subject stand out.

Brightness

Image brightness is something that gives a picture impact. If the picture lacks brightness it will have as much impact as a wet fish and, speaking of such, here's a picture of wet fish.

Step 1 The brightness control offers a range of between −100 and +100. As you move the slider, the image you're working on will adjust to show you the effect the brightness is having on the picture.

Step 2 You don't have to darken the whole picture. In this example, an oval marquee was made over the centre area of the image and inverted to cover the surrounding area. Then the brightness was reduced to darken the edges creating a dark vignette and placing emphasis on the centre of the picture.

The brightness control can be used selectively: here an oval marquee was used and the outer area made darker using the brightness control.

Blur/sharpen

Blur and sharpen tools are useful for emphasising an area or reducing its impact. You hold down the mouse button as you run over the pixels with the blur tool to soften the pixels and reduce that impact that area has. The sharpen tool has the opposite effect of enhancing edge definition to make the pixels stand out from the rest.

Use the blur tool to reduce spots and freckles, dust marks, to add a feeling of movement on tree leaves, or as a general background blur. It can also be used to reduce the high edge definition that some digital camera pictures have.

Use the sharpen tool to increase the surface texture of objects or the definition in parts of a picture. Sharpening a portraits eyes can have a powerful effect. Avoid going too far, however, because the edges will become too harsh and pixels will start to change colour with high contrast.

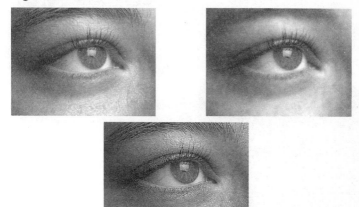

Left: Original picture. Right: The blur tool was used to soften around the eye. Bottom: The sharpen tool was used all over the picture.

Scratch removal

No matter how careful we are with negatives and transparencies some almost invariably become scratched. Equally when scanning in negatives that haven't been stored well you'll probably find the scanner picks up all the bits of dust that have settled on the film's surface.

These blemishes appear as white pixels and stand out like a sore thumb when you look at the scanned image on screen.

Depending on where the marks are, removing them can be a complicated task. There are a number of ways to approach this. The most obvious is the clone tool or rubber stamp.

Use the clone tool to pick pixels from a nearby area and clone them over the white or black speck or scratch.

Step 1 First, look at the scratch that you want to remove, then look around the picture for areas that have similar detail that you could use as the cloning source. In many cases pixels by the side of the scratch will do, but sometimes it's not that easy.

Step 2 Click on the alt button with the clone tool positioned over the area you want to sample then move the cursor over the scratch.

Now click on the mouse and move the cursor over the scratch. If you've sampled the right pixels the scratch will start to disappear and the new pixels will take its place. If the wrong pixels are sampled you'll see the scratch replaced by a row of pixels that stand out from the surrounds. Undo the action and resample pixels from a more appropriate area and try again.

Step 3 If you can't find any pixels to match the area that is covered by the scratch you may have to consider using a sample from another image. Open this and click on the area to be sampled then go to the damaged photo and start to clone over the scratch. It works just as though you are sampling from the same picture.

Cropping a picture

Cropping a picture is one of the simplest forms of image editing you can do. The crop tool looks like a pair of croppers used as a compositional aid by professional photographers – two L shaped pieces of card that are held over each other, and facing opposite directions, to form a window. As you slide the corners closer together the window becomes smaller and the crop tighter. The same happens on the PC: you click at one corner where you want to crop and drag the cursor to the opposite end. A set of 'marching ants' appears as a box shape and everything outside will be deleted if you click in the centre.

Left: The original may have too many distractions that can be removed to make a more pleasing picture. Try using the crop tool. Right: There, a better composition and a much smaller file size.

Using the crop tool removes unwanted background, saving file space, and makes more striking compositions.

Removing distractions

Take a picture of any historical building these days and it will no doubt include a telegraph pole or cables to spoil the authenticity of the shot. The clone tool can be used to remove the unwanted distractions. If a telegraph pole cuts through the building, clone from nearby using similar subject matter. If it's in the background try cloning from a nearby tree or sky to replace the pole. In this example, the bird of prey's perch is in the way. Use a brush size slightly larger than the width of the perch and then reduce this to work on the edges of the freshly cloned area if they can be seen.

Left: A decent picture, but wouldn't it be better without the post?
Right: By selecting similar surrounding pixels it's relatively easy to remove the post and clean up the background.

Removing someone from a picture

It's inevitable that relationships break down and, occasionally, you'll have a group photo that includes someone you'd no longer be seen dead with. They've just gotta go! Fortunately, we *can* change history and delete the individual – for good. If the person is at one side of the group it's easier to select a chunk of the background and copy and paste it inwards, covering as much of the person as you can. Then use the cloning tool to eat in at the rest of him, sampling from the background.

If he's in the middle of the picture, life becomes a little more complicated, but then that's what we'd expect anyway. Now you have two options: either remove him and slide the other group members inwards from either side to fill the gap, or cover him with background detail and have a gap. The latter may look too obvious so we'd go for the first option.

Top left: The woman on the middle right has to go.
Above: Draw roughly around the end person and copy and paste him onto another layer.
Bottom left: Use the erase on the new layer to rub out unwanted background and blend with the base layer.

There is one other thought. You could always scan in a famous celebrity and clone in his or her head over the offending person. Then you'd be in with the jet set!

10 | ADVANCED TECHNIQUES

This unit will help you get to grips with the more advanced image-editing techniques so you can really add impact to your pictures. Learn how to create a sense of speed, change the weather, make better selections, create new backgrounds and control depth of field. There's also a full explanation of blending modes. Let's start by finding out how to create a sensation of speed.

Creating movement

Capturing movement using a camera can be a difficult technique to master. It's a careful balance of the right shutter speed and the way the camera is handled. Slow shutter speeds are needed to ensure the subject looks as though it's moving, but then you risk introducing camera shake. Using a fast shutter speed to prevent camera shake will stop your subject in its tracks, but the risk is that the shot may look boring.

The best approach is to look through the camera and follow the subject along its path. As it moves in front of you, fire the shutter and continue to follow the subject as you hold the shutter button down. The result will be a sharp subject set against a blurred background. The shutter speed you use will affect the blurriness of the background; the longer, the more blurred. The knack is to balance the result so it obviously looks blurred but not enough so you can't tell what it is.

Fortunately, you don't have to worry about your camera technique as much now as most types of movement can be recreated using effects in your image-editing program. To illustrate this I've chosen a picture of a car shot at a racing circuit. The photograph, while technically fine, doesn't have any real feeling of speed, but it soon will have.

A digital picture looks fine when it's displayed at an acceptable size.

Look closely and you'll see the picture's made up of squares called pixels.

Pictures taken on digital cameras vary in quality depending on the camera's resolution. These three pictures show the effect of three categories of resolution.

This was taken on a Fuji DX-9 which has a 350,000 pixel CCD.

Here the Nikon Coolpix 950 with its 2.11 million pixel CCD was used.

The Minolta RD3000 captured this close up of the eye using a 3 million pixel image.

Adjusting the hue of a picture will result in very strange colour shifts that can be very effective.

These three strips show the effect that adjusting Saturation will have on an image.

Using Replace Colour it's possible to change any part of a picture, in this case the woman's jacket from red to blue.

It's easy to make a selection using the Colorise option in the Hue/Saturation palette.

Original picture can be changed using the lighting filter.

Here each of the windowpanes was first selected and an orange colour was added using the Hue and Saturation options. A spotlight lighting effect was then added to the upper window to make it look as though a light is on.

Convert a black & white image to CMYK.

All but the hair is masked so the hair can be coloured.

Each adjustment layer can be used to colour bits of the image.

Select the area you want to colour and create a mask. Then make a Curves Adjustment layer naming it so it's appropriate to the selection. Now select a colour channel and adjust its curve, watching the image on screen change colour. For realistic skin tones take out some cyan from the highlights and increase magenta and yellow.

Create a rainbow using the Gradient tool.

The end result – take your time and it will look as real as an original colour image.

Here two pictures of the rope and buildings were combined to ensure maximum depth of field.

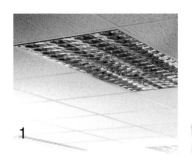

1

2

3

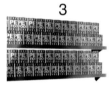

4

5

6

Each layer can be turned on and worked on individually, several layers can be flattened to reduce the file size, and layers can be grouped and edited as one.

Layers	Channels	Paths
Normal	⬦ Opacity:	
☐ Preserve Transparency		
👁		Edge of trolly
👁		cans in trolly
👁		right paw
👁		left paw
👁		trolly 5
👁		shadow of trolly 6
👁		dog 2
👁		sign
👁		base of dog
👁		Layer 5
👁		pet food stack 4
👁		cans stack 2 3
👁		background dog
👁		ceiling 1
👁		shadows
👁 ✏		*Background*

Digital PhotoFX designer, Chris Robinson, was commissioned by *Pet Product Marketing* magazine to create an illustration that would give an article about pet foods in supermarkets a more lively presentation. Chris shot the ceiling, shopping trolley and home-made pet food cans then combined them with the photo of the dog using a total of 15 layers.

Digital photography can also be used to create bizarre images, especially when you use the layers option.

Layers can be turned on or off as you build up the picture.

The original background with no extra layers turned on.

Turning on the second layer with Gaussian Blur and Diffuse glow set to around 50% results in a softer more ethereal image.

The third layer adds a graduated blue to the sky.

Painter's Clone mode can be used to clone back an image with a brush stroke effect.

The Clone mode of Metacreations Painter has a Tracing option that lets you draw over a knocked back original to make a sketch of it.

Play around with Adjustment Layers to create strange-coloured images.

Use Painter to create a Van Gogh effect automatically.

Photoshop's duotone mode allows subtle colour to be applied to a black & white image. Here adding blue, green and brown has produced three different toned images.

Using Goo can stretch and distort pictures – it has a comical effect when used on faces.

Use your flatbed scanner to scan in real objects such as this leaf. The background is the same leaf enlarged and made blurred. The leaf has a slight shadow to make it lift off the page.

Paint Shop Pro's Picture Tubes lets you paint objects onto the picture. Here the grass, fire and clouds were added from Tubes supplied with the program.

The Tapestry mode of MGI's PhotoSuite III lays pictures over an original to create a mosaic-style effect.

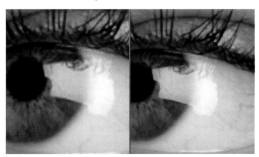

Using Genuine Fractals Photoshop plug-in allows pictures to be compressed to a tiny size and reopened to large file sizes with very little loss in quality.

Shoot several pictures and combine them to make fun images.
Here the Toy Story model was photographed on a white
background and combined with the boy's head and a Photoshop-
created background. The feet were blurred with motion blur to give
a feeling of movement.

Step 1 First, let's select around the car. The magnetic lasso or polygonal lasso tool can be used for this. Once you're happy select a one pixel feather and contract the selection by one pixel too. Now invert the selection so the background is picked.

Step 2 Apply a touch of motion blur, Filter>Blur>Motion Blur, making sure the angle matches the direction of the car. Experiment with the settings until you're happy with the degree of background blur.

Step 3 Now let's make the wheels spin. Select one using the freehand lasso and apply the radial blur filter, Filter>Blur>Radial Blur. Start with a small number and undo and try again if you're unhappy with the result. Set the effect to spin, not zoom.

Step 4 You may want to add a bit of smoke around the tyres so it looks as though they're burning round the track. Open a new canvas and apply, Filter>Render>Clouds, using black and white for foreground and background colours. Take a sample from the clouds using the clone tool and move to the racing car picture to apply the cloned sample. Easy!

Adding a graduated sky

The contrast between the ground and sky can often be too much for a camera's metering system, so you often have to choose between a well exposed foreground and a pale sky or a great sky and a dark foreground. Some experienced photographers get round the problem by using a graduated filter over the lens to bring the sky closer in exposure to the ground. These filters are available in a wide range of colours and some are much more natural than others.

It's also very easy to add any colour you like in Photoshop. When you take the picture expose for the foreground and add the sky.

Step 1 Use the magic wand tool to select the white sky. If it doesn't pick up the whole lot in one go, either increase the tolerance setting or hold down the alt key and click on another part to add to the selection.

Step 2 When all the sky is selected select a one to three pixel feather and, to ensure you don't get a white edge around the skyline, expand the selection by one or two pixels.

Step 3 Go to the gradient tool and select the linear version. Choose foreground to background or foreground to transparent and the multiply blend mode. Make sure the foreground colour is set to the colour you want the sky to appear and the background colour either a weaker version or white.

Step 4 Place the cursor at the top of the picture, click and hold down as you drag the mouse to the skyline. Let go and a graduated colour will appear.

Step 5 If it's not how you wanted it, undo and try again.

Tip

There is a more natural, but fiddly option. Take two pictures – one exposed for the ground the other for the sky – and combine the two digitally to get a perfect result.

Step by step graduated sky. If you don't feather and contract the selection you'll see a white outline around the trees. Feathering done, and no white line. The end result is looking good!

Making selections

One of the most challenging parts of image editing is making selections. Do it wrong and your image will look like a poor cardboard cut out.

Here are a few tips to help you make a better edge.

Use the polygonal lasso on straight edges. Click at one end and move to the next part along the straight edge. Click again to create a line that can be moved using the cursor as a positioning tool. Let go and the first part of the selection is complete. Continue working your way around until you meet up back where you started. Click the mouse to form the loop.

If any areas are too bendy use the freehand lasso with the shift key to add to the selection or the alt key to take away. If you forget which key does what, look at the symbol on screen by the lasso icon.

When the edge you want to select is clearly defined use the magic lasso which does a great job of keeping track of and selecting edges.

Photoshop 5.5 also has an extract filter that can be used to make complex selections, Image>Extract. You first paint around the edge and when you make a loop fill the middle of the selection. Then the program detects where the edge is and removes the background.

Use the magic wand tool when the area you want to select is a similar tone. Start with a low tolerance setting and click on a sample area. Similar pixels will then be selected. If selected pixels also appear in unwanted areas you can either reduce the tolerance setting or deselect the unrequired pixels by drawing round them with the freehand lasso while holding down the alt key.

If too few pixels are selected, hold down the shift key and click a new area using the magic wand tool or increase the tolerance setting.

If your program allows the image to be split into individual colour channels, view them individually to see if the area you want to select is more defined in one of them. If so, make the selection in the single channel and revert back to the full colour image to cut it out.

Make an adjustment layer, Layer>New>Adjustment Layer, and adjust the curves until the subject that you want to select is more of a contrast against its background.

Photoshop 5.5's magic eraser makes easy work of cut outs – just click around your image to remove unwanted areas that are left as transparent areas.

The background eraser is almost as easy – as you drag along an edge it automatically selects a background and makes it transparent so it isn't seen when you copy and paste.

Draw around the subject with the brush in Extract mode.

You can view the image on a black background in extract mode to make sure it will work when pasted into the destination image.

MGI PhotoSuite has a useful edge finder that you drag over the edge of your selection – it looks at both sides of the edge and calculates where the selection should be made.

Changing backgrounds

There are many occasions when the choice of background is well out of our control. Situations such as an old statue in the street with a modern shop firmly in the distance; or a model at a show with various trade stands in the way. Your partner in the pub in a dimly lit room or a bird with a branch growing out of the back of its head. These are all examples that can be improved by changing the background. The skill is in changing the background so it still looks natural; otherwise, it can alter the whole feel of the picture.

Step 1 Make the selection – this can be difficult if the subject has fine edge detail. Use the magic wand if the subject has a similar range of tones around the edge. If not use a pen tool or lasso and enlarge the picture on screen to magnify the detail.

Step 2 When it's all selected, add a one or two pixel feather and contract by one pixel, Select>Modify>Contract. Copy the selection.

Step 3 Choose a suitable background and resize if necessary so that it matches the image you're going to use with it. Paste so that the original selection appears on the background and use the transform tool to resize if necessary. I've also added a shadow.

If you've done a good job it will be difficult to see the joins. Do a bad job and you may have a trace or two of the original background. These can be removed using the eraser providing you haven't flattened the image. If so use the clone tool and sample from near the edge onto the edge.

Using layers

Having access to layers is great, as it is one of the most powerful tools that a program can have. Many low priced programs have a similar feature but call them objects. A layer is like a sheet of glass containing part of a picture. They can be laid on top of one another to create a complete picture. Each layer can be moved individually and adjusted without affecting the rest. Photoshop and Paint Shop Pro also use blend modes that affect how the pixels in one layer react with the next. More about these later.

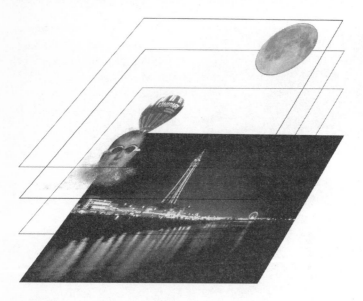

Try to imagine layers as sheets of acetate. This is what they would look like if you lifted them away from one another.

Layers can be used to mix sections of a picture and fade areas while blending others. You can add text, graphics and pictures combining them in an artistic way and make montages with ease.

Adjustment layers

Photoshop and Paint Shop Pro have a superb feature called adjustment layers that makes it easier to fine control parts of the image. An adjustment layer can be used to adjust elements such as the colour, saturation and brightness of the image even with levels and curves controls. It can then be left on or switched off without affecting the things you've done before or after the layer was introduced. You can also make an adjustment layer of just a selected part of the image to fine tune components in a picture. If, for example, you have a picture of a bowl of fruit you could set up adjustment layers for each item in the bowl and return to any layer to control just the colour and saturation of that particular piece of fruit.

Adjustment layers were used here so that various parts of the woman's face could be individually hand coloured. (See colour plate 6.)

Using blend modes

Programs such as Photoshop and Paint Shop Pro 6 have a set of blend modes that work with layers. Each layer can be assigned a blend mode that changes the way pixels in the active layer react with the ones in the layers below.

Using blend modes is very much a case of trial and error at first until you become familiar with the characteristics of each mode.

Here's a brief run down of the effect each has on the picture.

Normal

This default mode is not affected by the base image when the active layer is set at 100% so the pixels produce the end colour. If you change the opacity of the active layer colours blend with the layer below to form an average of the two.

Dissolve

This mode has no effect on the image unless the active layer has been feathered and then a splattering effect appears in the feathered area producing dissolved colours.

Multiply

The active layer takes pixels from the layer below and adds them to its own producing a darker picture. Black areas will stay black while the colours below will affect light areas.

Screen

Opposite effect to multiply with the end colour always appearing lighter. Black areas of the active layer stay unchanged while white areas lighten.

Overlay

Similar to multiply, but overlay keeps the base colour's highlights and shadows while mixing with the active layer to produce an image with more contrast.

Soft light

Similar to overlay, but more subtle. If the blend colour is lighter than 50% grey, the whole image will lighten. If it's darker than 50% grey, the image will darken. How much depends on the paint colour used. When you merge layers you benefit from a lighter image.

Hard light

This adds colours together and, like soft light, lightens the image if lighter than 50% grey, and darkens the blend colour if it's already darker than 50% grey. The effect is a harsher version of the overlay mode.

Colour dodge

Uses the upper layer to add colour and brighten the base layer's colours. Blending with black doesn't affect the image.

Colour burn

Merges the darker colours of the upper active layer with the layer below. Blending with white has no affect on the overall image.

Darken

Selects the darker of the base or active layer as the final colour. Lighter pixels are replaced – darker pixels stay the same.

Lighten

Looks at the colour in each layer and selects the lighter of the base or blend layer as the final colour. Pixels darker than the blend colour are replaced, and lighter pixels stay the same.

Difference

Looks at which colour has the brightest value and subtracts the weaker. Blending with white inverts the base colour, but black has no affect.

Exclusion

A similar, but lower contrast effect than the difference mode.

Hue

Produces a combined colour that includes the luminance and saturation of the base colour and the hue of the active layer's colour.

Saturation

Takes the hue and luminance of the base colour and blends it with the saturation of the active layer's colour.

Colour

Produces an end colour with the luminance of the base colour and the hue and saturation of the blend colour.

Luminosity

Mixes hue and saturation of the base colour and the luminance of the active layer's colour to create the opposite effect of colour mode.

Using quick mask mode

Quick mask is a technique borrowed from the printing industry. When areas of an image had to be masked to avoid appearing in print the repro house or typesetter would mask off the area of film using a red opaque varnish. All areas under the varnish would be protected from the printing process. A similar varnish effect can be applied to an image in quick mask mode which is also known as ruby mask in some programs.

Quick mask mode was used to select the statue from its background.

The red area of pixels is painted on using a brush and the original image can still be seen through the mask. The idea is to fill in a large area using a large brush then work on the detailed edges using a small brush. If you make a mistake and go too far over the edge you can erase the mask using the eraser tool, again set to large for big areas and small for detail. Once an area has been masked you can turn it into a selection ready for editing.

Controlling depth of field

Depth of field is the term used to describe the amount of sharp focus in front and behind the subject. A shallow depth of field will have the subject plane sharp, but everything in front and behind quickly going out of focus. This technique is often used to make the subject stand out from the background or reduce the effect of distracting foreground detail.

Wedding photographers often use shallow depth of field to blur flowers in the foreground giving a pleasing frame or border to the portrait. Fashion photographers use the same technique to throw the catwalk background out of focus so our eye settles on the model and, more importantly, the clothing.

At the opposite end of the scale, if you're photographing a landscape with a tree in the foreground and a distant mountain you want it all in focus, so maximum depth of field is required. Similarly, a holiday shot of your partner standing in front of, say, the Taj Mahal won't look very good if either the person, or one of the wonders of the world, is out of focus.

Photographers control depth of field in traditional cameras by adjusting the aperture. A wide aperture reduces the depth of field while a small aperture increases it. With most digital and 35 mm compact cameras you have no control and have to accept what the camera does in the available conditions.

Fortunately, the digital image maker can do things on the computer. By selecting certain areas of the picture it's possible to blur the background to make it look out of focus and give the impression of shallow depth of field. And, while it's not possible to sharpen up a really blurred picture there is a way to increase depth of field. Let's look at both options, starting with reducing depth of field.

Step 1 We've already covered making selections earlier in the book so first choose a suitable photograph and make a selection around the subject you want sharp. Copy this and paste onto a new layer.

Step 2 Turn off the background layer and, with the new cut out layer active, use the eraser to remove any bits of remaining background that are on the edges of the cut out.

Step 3 Turn the background layer back on, make it active and turn the cut out layer off. If you went ahead and blurred the background the original area that you've cut out will spread into the background and may result in a coloured halo around the cut out. To avoid this use the clone tool on the background layer to pick up the area around the cut out and clone over the edges of it.

Step 4 Call up the Gaussian blur option and adjust the controls watching the preview to see what effect it has on the selected background. If you can't see an area you're working on either click on the preview window and drag to move the magnified section to the area you want or click on the reducing square to see a less magnified preview. This slows down the effect on the preview, but lets you see more of the overall image.

Step 5 Apply the filter and view the result. Look at it magnified and at full screen to make sure you're happy. If not, undo the filter and try again. If you're happy flatten the result and save.

Now to increase depth of field. In many cases the sharpening filter can improve a picture but it won't bring an out-of-focus area back to life. The way to do this, if you can't control the aperture on the camera, is to take two pictures from the same viewpoint, one focusing on the foreground subject the other on the background. Then, when the results are scanned in on the computer, merge the two together using the cut out techniques covered earlier.

In the following examples even the camera's manual control set to the smallest aperture didn't allow the depth of field that was required to ensure the nearby rope was in focus along with the distant harbour scene. So two pictures were taken and the pair combined.

Step 1
Open both images.

Step 2 Then copy one and paste it into the other. Adjust the height so that both sets of buildings appear roughly in the same area. Set the opacity to a low percentage so you can see the layer below to help position the new layer.

Step 3 Once in place choose add a Layer>Mask Layer>Add Layer Mask>Reveal All.

Step 4 Then select the gradient tool, set it to foreground to background and draw a line from the base of the boats to just above the rope. The two images will now combine flawlessly without any joins. (See colour plate 7.)

Hand colouring

Scanning in a black & white image and hand colouring it can produce great looking effects. Try adding pastel colours to recreate an old-fashioned hand-coloured style.

Step 1 Convert the black & white image to CMYK.

Step 2 Make a selection around an area that you want to colour.

Step 3 Press Q with the selection active to create a mask around the selection.

Step 4 Press Control+I to inverse the selection and use the brush to paint on more mask and the eraser to remove mask to ensure it's covering the selection exactly. Press Control+I to revert back to the original selection.

Step 5 Use Gaussian blur at a low setting to give a soft edge to the mask.

Step 6 Exit quick mask mode by pressing Q and make an adjustment layer, Layer>New>Adjustment Layer. Select Curves as the adjustment option and give the layer a name that's appropriate to the selection; in our case, face.

Step 7 Now select one of the colour channels and adjust its curve, watching the image on screen change colour. For realistic skin tones take out some cyan from the highlights and increase magenta and yellow.

Step 8 Repeat these steps for other parts of the image.

Unsharp Mask

Oddly, the name doesn't really refer to what this image editing function does. Applying an unsharp mask makes the picture sharper by increasing the contrast on edge areas of pixels.

Several programs have an unsharp mask and they usually have a fair amount of control to allow the best use of sharpening.

The original scan is quite soft.

Apply too much sharp mask and the picture will start to look unnatural.

Use the fade command or reduce sharpness value to improve the photo.

11 SPECIAL EFFECTS

Digital photography has the power to unleash the creative side of your mind. With the right ideas and the software tools anything's possible. In this unit we'll look at a range of ideas that you could use to change your pictures.

Rendering flare

Flare is one of those annoying things that crops up when you wish it hadn't. It's the result of light passing through the lens and reflecting off the internal glass elements. The problem is most noticeable when the sun is in, or just out of, the frame. When the light's at this angle it's easy for it to bounce around inside the lens. The result will be a series of bright shapes covering the image. Sometimes it will be a large single shape, and other times just a streak of flare. In both instances the overall contrast of the picture is reduced.

Flare can be used to add a sparkling highlight to part of a subject. Here it's made the potato a little more symbolic!

Lens manufacturers can reduce the problem by improving the optical construction and coating of the glass. You can help by altering the viewpoint, screwing a hood onto the lens or shielding the lens using your hand. Of course you could decide to leave the flare there because it can make a picture more striking. For this reason several programs have a flare filter that introduces the very thing we've all been trying to get rid of.

The advantage of being able to create flare manually is that it can be placed anywhere within the picture and can be controlled to be powerful or subtle. None of this is really possible with a traditional camera.

Photoshop's flare filter can be found by going to, Filter>Render> Lens Flare.

Here you're greeted with a pop-up preview that has a brightness control and a choice of three lens options. Place the cursor on the part of the picture where you want the flare to occur and click. The result appears quickly and from here you can decide whether to change the lens or the strength of the flare.

Picture Publisher 8 has much more controllable flare, found in the Effects menu. Its palette has options to adjust all aspects of flare including the flare itself and its halo, reflection and rays, by changing the brightness, glow, length and direction.

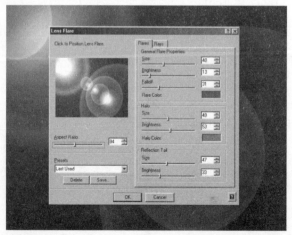

Picture Publisher's flare feature offers more control than Photoshop's.

Making a rainbow

Paint the world with a rainbow – it's easy with a gradient editor. Photoshop, Paint Shop Pro and Photo-Paint have one of these which allows all types of graduated effect to be added to a picture. Making a rainbow is easy, watch.

Step 1 Open up a picture that you'd like a rainbow to appear on and make a new layer.

Step 2 Click on the gradient tool (flood fill in Paint Shop Pro (PSP)) and select the radial option (Sunburst Gradient in PSP) from the sub-menu.

Step 3 Double-click to bring up the gradient palette and select transparent rainbow (fading spectrum in PSP).

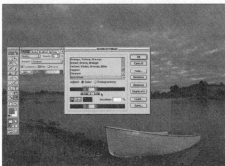

Step 4 Now click on edit and drag all the colours closer together using the little triangles that appear under the coloured bar. Set them at 2% apart.

Step 5 Add a new triangle at each side of the rainbow colours and change the colour to black so the rainbow is surrounded with black.

Step 6 Create a new layer and call it rainbow. Make the picture small on screen and allow space in the window around the canvas. With the gradient tool selected, click in the window outside the canvas to the left or right below the canvas, depending on which way you want the rainbow to arc. Hold the mouse down and drag across the picture and when you're near the top let go. The rainbow will appear. At this stage it will be black around the rainbow covering the original image: don't worry, we'll sort that next. If the shape or position of the rainbow isn't right, click undo and try again.

Step 7 When you're happy with the positioning go to Gaussian blur and set it to about 40 pixels to soften the colours of the rainbow.

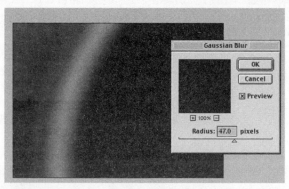

Step 8 Go to the layers blend mode and set screen mode and reduce the opacity to about 60%. Now the black will disappear and the rainbow will look naturally placed.

Step 9 You may want to remove areas of the rainbow that would look more natural if they were behind the subject. Either carefully erase these pieces out or clone the subject back from the background layer, or, if you're lucky enough to have Photoshop 5 with its history brush, use that to paint areas of the picture back to the previous state. (See colour plate 6.)

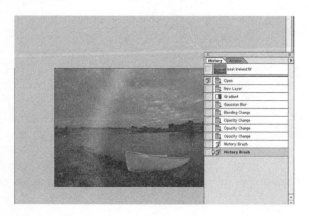

Rendering clouds

Photoshop has a useful clouds creating filter but it's not as impressive as the version that comes with the Xenofex plug-in effects from Alien Skin.

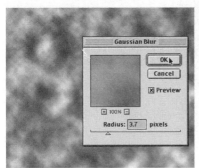

Step 1 Creating clouds using the foreground and background colours is easy with either of these programs and the results can be used to fill in a dull sky that you may have on one of your landscapes or as a background to a portrait that currently has a distracting one.

Step 2 With Photoshop the clouds are placed over your existing photograph so you should make a new layer and render the clouds on there. Then use the copy and paste to take a selection onto the clouds layer.

Xenofex's cloud filter has much more control and lays the clouds over the existing picture, but if you want them as a background you can still save them onto a new layer.

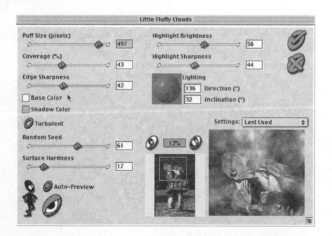

With Xenofex you have the option of adjusting the size, frequency and rendomness of the clouds as well as their opacity.

Creating a galaxy

Photoshop and similar packages can be used to create star filled galaxies. Start with a black canvas.

Step 1 Open a new document and fill with black.

Step 2 Then add the stars using the noise filter set to Gaussian and monochromatic, Filter>Add Noise.

Step 3 Use, Image>Adjust>Threshold, to reduce the number of stars.

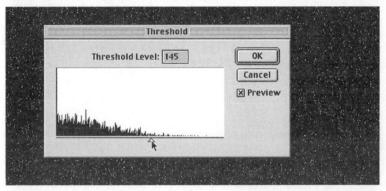

Step 4 Blur them slightly to avoid the harsh points.

Step 5 Add some flare, Filter>Render>Lens Flare. (See colour plate 16.)

Create night star trails

Leave a camera pointing up at the night sky with the shutter open for the duration and you'll create star trails as the earth rotates on its axis. Emulate this digitally by repeating steps 1 to 4 of the galaxy technique and then apply radial blur with the setting on spin and best quality. Adjust brightness and contrast to ensure the trail stands out from the black background.

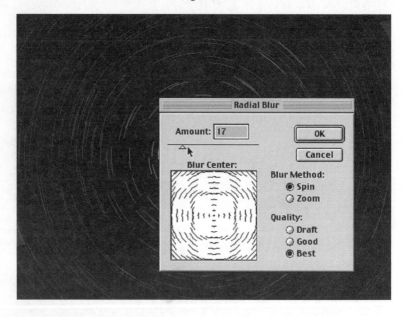

Create snow

It's quite easy to add a blizzard to an image.

Step 1 Choose a suitable picture and create a new layer.

Step 2 Fill the layer with white, Edit>Fill, making sure the foreground is set to white.

Step 3 Add noise, Filter>Noise>Add Noise, and select Gaussian mode and monochromatic.

Step 4 Add motion blur, Filter>Blur> Motion Blur. Select an appropriate angle for the snow to fall at and the length of the strokes.

Step 5 Adjust image contrast so the streaks appear black against a white background.

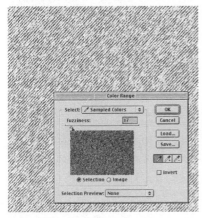

Step 6 Go to, Select>Colour Range, and adjust the fuzziness slider to around 100 so that all the black appears selected. Invert the selection if you've picked up a white area.

Step 7 Press the delete key to remove the black and leave the streaks of white snow.

Step 8 Make the streaks slightly blurred using the blur or Gaussian blur filter.

Step 9 Set to overlay blend mode to give a really icy snow effect.

Add ripples to water

Creating the effect after a stone has just being thrown in water is a doddle.

Step 1 Make a selection of the area you want the ripple to affect. In this case a circular marquee was made. Apply the zigzag filter from the, Filter>Distort, sub-menu. Set it to pond ripple and adjust the slider until the strength of rings is correct for the image you're working on.

Step 2 The ripple has also affected the buoy so you could either undo the effect and use the lasso with minus selected to remove the buoy before applying the ripple or, if you have Photoshop with its history brush, you could brush back the original image. This is what I did here.

Recreate an infrared image

Black & white infrared pictures can be taken on digital cameras providing you use a proper R72 infrared filter over the lens. Alternatively, here's a technique that can simulate the effect digitally using Adobe Photoshop.

Step 1 First convert your image to greyscale if it's colour and copy it onto a new layer.

Step 2 Apply the Gaussian blur filter.

Step 3 Now apply, Filter> Distort>Diffuse Glow, setting graininess to low, glow amount to high and the clear amount to around 6.

Step 4 Set the blend mode to hard light and reduce the opacity to around 80%, so the original base layer starts to show through.

Step 5 Experiment with the settings until you see infrared's characteristic glow where the green leaves were.

Posterization

This effect reduces the image into several colours giving a poster-style image. Traditional darkroom users would struggle to obtain this sort of effect using lith film and loads of patience. With Photoshop it's just a case of selecting how many levels/or colours you want. Somewhere between three and seven is adequate.

The left half of the picture is the full-tone image; the right shows what happens when a four-level posterisation is selected.

Crazy colours

This technique, that involves using adjustment layers in Photoshop, is perfect if you're after bizarre coloured images:

Step 1 Choose a suitable subject with a good shape. This car with the logos in the background is perfect.

Step 2 With the layer palette open select new adjustment layer from the menu under the small triangle at the top of the palette. Set the mode to inverse.

Step 3 Set the blend mode to difference.

Step 4 Drag the adjustment layer to the new layer icon to copy it and repeat this so you have three adjustment layers, and a wacky coloured image.

Step 5 The colour effect is probably too harsh and etched looking. Go to the original image layer and add Gaussian blur watching the preview until the effect is just how you want it. This smoothes out the colours. Go too far and you'll end up with an abstract colour scheme that could be used as a background to a collage or desktop pattern.

Experiment with adjustment layers to get effects like this. (See colour plate 11.)

Rendering lighting

If you can't master lighting using traditional equipment you can have a go after the picture's taken using the lighting effects that are available from programs such as Photoshop and Picture Publisher. From here you can apply lighting in various forms, shapes, brightness and colour to create spot effects, stage lighting, subtle room light, diffused sunlight and much more.

First, open up a suitable picture then select the lighting you want to try. Photoshop has a preview window and several sliders to control various aspects of the light. Move these around as you watch the effect in the preview window. Dragging the lighting icon around the preview window can alter the angle or position. (See colour plate 5.)

An okay picture, but I wanted a harsh sunlight effect.

Photoshop's lighting filter to the rescue! With a little care the lighting can look natural.

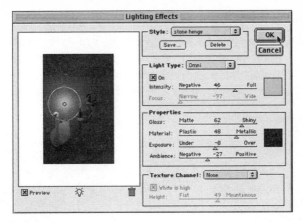

Two-faced

Taking a head on portrait and copying one half and pasting it onto the same half is a technique that's been achieved in the darkroom – with patience! With your image-editing program it's just a case of copying half, flipping it and moving the new layer into place. Use the arrow keys to move the selection around until it matches well and flatten the layers.

It's surprising how different two halves of a face can be. In some cases the results of two left sides are so dramatically different to two right sides that it could be a different person. In this example there's not so much difference. Oh, the pride of being father to a perfect son!

Take an image, cut it in half and sandwich the two left halves together... and the two right halves to create two very different people!

Alien Skin Xenofex

We've seen the effect of Xenofex's clouds filter but that's just one of 16 tricks up this fantastic plug-ins sleeve. It is compatible to run with Photoshop, Paint Shop Pro, Picture Publisher and Photo-Paint to give a range of interesting effects. Here's what you can expect.

Baked earth

Creates a crazed pattern like dried-up mud. You can control the length and width of cracks as well as the roughness of the edges. You also control the brightness and sharpness of the highlights and the light direction and angle to vary the depth of cracks.

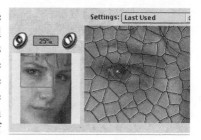

Constellation

This filter needs a fair amount of practice before you can make any use out of it. Master the controls and you'll recreate your images as points of light, making some subjects look like (as the name suggests) constellations. You can adjust the star size, sharpness and brightness.

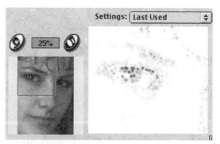

Crumple

Makes the subject look as though it's printed on crumpled paper. You can control the crinkle size, the depth of crinkle and the light direction and angle.

Distress

Creates an eroded look to text and edges of images. Options include edge width, irregularity and the type of edge.

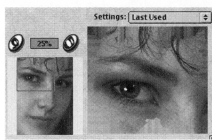

Electricity

A fantastic filter that recreates lightning around a subject. You have loads of control to change the length, spacing, glow width and colour, jaggedness, branches and meander. It works best around selections.

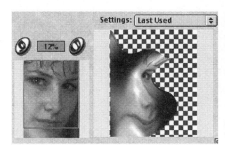

Flag

Makes the image appear like a flag, waving in the wind. Controls are available to adjust ripple thickness and strength as well as light direction and highlight brightness and sharpness.

Lightning

Creates forks of lightning across your picture and has the same range of adjustments as electricity.

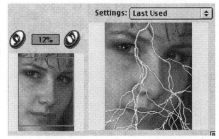

Little clouds

Used to make clouds with control available to adjust size, coverage, edge sharpness, turbulence and lighting direction.

Origami

Makes the image look as though it has been folded and unfolded by splitting it into small triangles that appear creased.

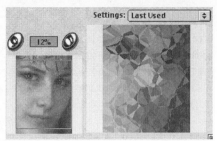

Puzzle

Places the pattern of a jigsaw over the image. You can select the number of columns and rows, the bevel width and light direction.

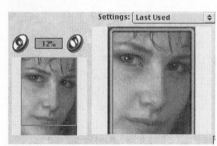

Rounded rectangle

Adds a rectangle with rounded corners on the inside of a selection. You can choose the colour size, thickness and light direction.

Shatter

Images appear as though they are viewed through broken glass.

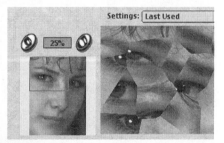

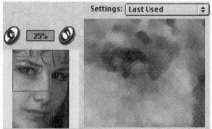

Shower door

Makes the image appear as though it's being viewed through patterned glass.

Stain

Create coffee cup stains and spillages using this filter.

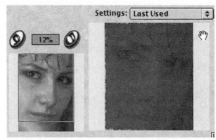

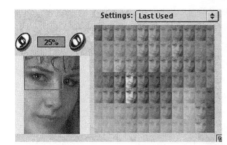

Stamper

Fills the image with thumbnails of the same image.

Television

Makes the image look as if it is being viewed on a badly tuned TV. You can adjust scanline strength and thickness, the curvature, add static and control ghost strength and breakup.

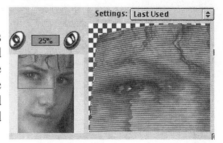

Artistic filters

Photoshop's range of artistic filters is a valuable feature of the program if you want to change the way your picture looks. To alter the effect you have various controls such as brush size and detail, texture, smoothness, light direction, relief, stroke length and colour. Some effects don't work very well when applied, but can be tweaked using the filter fade command.

The set of filters includes the following.

Coloured Pencil

Draws a rough crosshatch effect over the image using coloured pencils. The background image shows through the pencil strokes and important edges are held.

Cut out

Makes the image look as though it has been created using various pieces of torn paper by applying a posterising effect.

Dry brush.

Dry Brush

A dry-brush effect that makes the image look like a cross between an oil and watercolour painting.

Film Grain

Applies a pattern of grain across the image to make it look like a real photograph taken on fast film.

Fresco.

Fresco

Uses short, rounded, and quickly applied brush dabs to create a coarse stippled effect over the image.

Neon Glow

Adds a coloured glow to parts of the image.

Paint Daubs

Does what the name suggests. You can vary the brush size between 1 and 50 and choose simple, light rough, light dark, wide sharp, wide blurry and sparkle styles.

Palette Knife

Emulates a palette knife-style of painting.

Plastic wrap.

Plastic Wrap

Coats the image with a shiny plastic effect making it look like an ice sculpture.

Poster Edges

Creates arty poster effects by dramatically reducing the number of colours in the image and adding black lines around edges.

Rough Pastels

Makes the image look like it's on a textured background, covered in coloured pastel chalk strokes.

Smudge Stick

Adds diagonal stokes of smeared, or smudged, pixels across the image.

Sponge

Makes the image appear as though it has been painted using a sponge.

Underpainting

Adds a textured background to the image that shows through the surface.

Some effects don't work very well when applied but can be tweaked using the fade filter command. In the picture on the left underpainting looks awful, but when fade is set to 55% along with lighten blend mode we've created a very different and pleasing effect.

Watercolour

Simplifies image detail to give a watercolour painting effect. Use fade and blend modes to alter the effect.

Textures

Filter>Stylize>Extrude

Throws out blocks that look like cityscapes from above, each with the image pixels on the ends. Can be used quite effectively but don't overdo.

Filter>Texture>Stained Glass

Another interesting effect that puts a stained glass window style pattern over the image. Here I've used fade and darken blend mode to alter the effect.

Other plug-ins

There are many other plug-in filter packs available to expand programs such as Photoshop, Paint Shop Pro and PhotoPaint. The most popular are Kai's Power Tools and the Andromeda series, but hunt around on the Web and you'll find some great sites offering free or shareware plug-ins. One of the best sources for these is:

<http://www.netins.net/showcase/wolf359/plugcomm.html>

Here you'll find links to just about every plug-in supplier and loads of freebies too. Also try:

<http://www.perso.club-internet.fr/gpl/html/two_moon.html>

for similar information.

12 | SAVING PICTURES

When you've spent time creating a digital picture you'll want to save it to look at, share, print or store in the future. Digital pictures can take up a fair amount of space on your computer's hard drive so you have to consider alternative storage. We'll look at this in Unit 14, but first you need to decide what format to save the pictures in. With dozens to choose from it's easy to become unclear about the options. In this unit we'll look at all the formats and suggest ones you should use and why.

The format that an image is stored in can have an effect on the result. Some may compress the picture and remove detail to keep the file size small, some can't be read by certain programs and others are only compatible with one or two programs. Windows automatically adds a three- to four-letter extension at the end of the file when an image is saved on a PC. This can be set to be added on a Mac providing it's running on OS8.5. A PC will not recognise the file if you don't include the extension at the end so make sure you key it in if your computer doesn't automatically add one.

Most programs have their own custom file formats, known as native formats, to ensure certain exclusive features keep attached to the image. These formats tend to open more quickly within the program, too.

Major native formats

.psd

Photoshop saves pictures in .psd format and this can only be read by the more advanced image-editing programs. It saves in this format to keep layers separate so you can work on them in the future. If you try and save an image comprising layers in any other format Photoshop brings up a message that asks if you want to flatten the layers. If you want to keep an image with active layers it's safer to do a Save As and rename the file. You'll now have two copies – one with layers and one that other programs can read.

.ppf

Picture Publisher's own file format.

.cpt

Corel has a similar method of working and saves pictures as .cpt format. Other programs cannot read these files.

.psp

Paint Shop Pro saves files as .psp format that can contain layers, masks and alpha channels. This format has the option of selecting lossy or lossless compression to make the file size smaller.

Interchange formats

In a sharing world it makes sense to have a format that others will be able to open and view and there are several, known as interchange formats, and in no particular order.

.jpg

The most common is JPG (JPEG, pronounced jay peg, short for Joint Photographic Experts Group). This format can be read by any image-editing program, exported into desktop publishing software and used on Web sites. It's a lossy compression format that means it loses data to reduce the size of the file. The compression level is variable in a scale from 0 to 10 so you can decide whether to have a low compression and large file size or high compression and small file size. At high compression much of the data is removed to maintain the small file size. This is returned when you open the picture but the quality is often poor. Aim to save pictures at around 7 upward for the best quality.

Most digital cameras write the pictures as JPEGs to allow more pictures to be taken using the camera's memory.

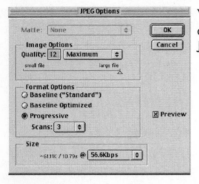

You can select the level of compression when saving a JPEG image.

Progressive JPEG is similar to JPEG but designed for use on Web pages as it opens as a low resolution version initially and, as the name implies, progressively works up to a high resolution version. The benefit to viewers is they can choose early on whether to bother waiting to see the final image saving on phone bills and time.

.tif

Tiff is also a very popular format. Short for tagged image file format. These can be compressed but don't lose any picture information – known as lossless compression. The compressed file is bigger than a JPEG and slower to open than a native format, but the compromise is worth it for the quality and the fact that it's widely accepted by most programs.

If you intend sending pictures to be published you will find most repro houses prefer this format.

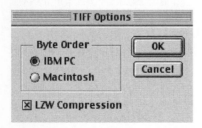

.bmp

Bitmap is the standard Windows format that supports RGB, index colours, greyscale and bitmaps. It doesn't support alpha channels, layers or CMYK images, but can be read by most programs.

.pict

Used by Mac computers and supports RGB images in any bit depth with one alpha channel. If Quicktime is installed files can be saved in four levels of JPEG compression. Some PC based programs such as Corel Photo-Paint can read PICT files but not many others.

.pcd

Kodak designed the PhotoCD format for transferring slides and negatives onto CD and five versions of each picture are scanned and saved to disk. The user has the option of opening a small 128 × 192 pixel image, with a file size of just 72 K, or any one of the other four other sizes up to the largest 2048 × 3072 pixels at 18 Mb, depending on the requirement of the picture.

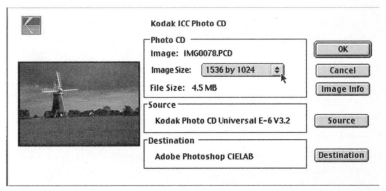

A PhotoCD image can be opened at different sizes and using different profiles to ensure it matches exact requirements.

The files are PICTs with RGB colour and 100 different images can be held on a disk. There's also a Pro PhotoCD that adds a sixth file size of 4096 × 6144 pixels at 72 Mb. This CD holds just 25 images.

The scanned images can look a little flat and often need boosting to improve contrast. It's not a format that you can save to – only pro labs or bureaux have the necessary equipment to write to this format and it costs about £1 per image for PhotoCD versions and £10 for the Pro PhotoCD option.

.eps

A file usually associated with drawing or layout packages as it saves vector graphics as well as standard images using postscript language. When opening a file in an image-editing program the vector is converted into bitmap and you have a choice of how big you want the image to appear. The image resolution is only dependent on the output device. EPS doesn't support clipping paths or alpha channels, but it does support Lab, CMYK and RGB colours.

.fpx

FlashPix is another format developed by Kodak along with Live Picture, Microsoft and Hewlett-Packard. Like PhotoCD it's a multi-resolution format that is selected automatically by the software as the image is viewed at different sizes. The benefit is that only the part of image displayed on screen is running on the active memory so editing becomes faster. Any changes you make are recorded as a script that can then be applied to the whole image at any of the sizes.

Most programs can't read or write to this format, but Kodak supply a plug-in for Photoshop.

.png

The successor to GIF, PNG (Portable Network Graphics) is used to transmit and store bitmap images. It allows 24-bit and 36-bit colour and can be set to progressive viewing. It has better compression than GIF. As the format is fairly new not every program supports it yet.

.gif

CompuServe GIF, or Graphics Interchange Format, is one of the most popular image formats for use on the Internet. It uses LZW compression and reduces the colour range to just 256 colours. Some programs show a palette with the colours being used along with a preview image so you can decide whether to save as a GIF or stick with a more flexible JPEG.

Two versions are available – GIF87a and GIF89a. The latter allows transparent pixels to be included when saved. Gifs can be saved in a variety of palettes to suit the Web browser.

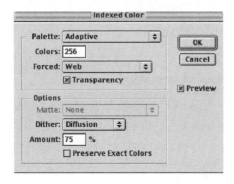

.iff

Interchange File Format used by Amiga and not that popular these days.

.pdf

Short for Portable Document Format. This is normally used to convert QuarkXPress documents to an electronic format that any computer can read using Acrobat Reader, which is freely available. The benefit is that pictures, words and graphics can be viewed exactly as they were created on Mac or PC platforms, even if the viewer doesn't have the correct fonts or picture files on the computer. (.pdf files can be saved with JPEG compression.) There seems little reason to save an individual image to this format, however. So avoid.

.tga

Truevision Targa is designed for use with systems using a Truevision video board. It's mainly used on the PC platform by professionals using video animation combined with graphics and supports 32-bit images in RGB with an 8-bit alpha channel.

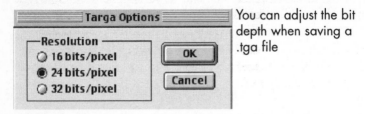

You can adjust the bit depth when saving a .tga file

As a matter of interest, Table 12.1 shows how photo size varies when saved in different formats.

File format	Size
Native Photoshop PSD	8.9 Mb
TIFF	11 Mb
TIFF with lossless compression	3.8 Mb
JPEG maximum quality 12	1.3 Mb
JPEG high quality 9	340 K
JPEG medium quality 7	216 K
JPEG low quality 4	132 K
JPEG low quality 0	76 K
Progressive JPEG	1.1 Mb
EPS	14.9 Mb
BMP	11 Mb
PICT	8.9 Mb
Photoshop PDF	1.7 Mb
GIF 256 colours	1.6 Mb

Table 12.1 An 11 Mb RGB image will change in size (as indicated in the table below) when saved in different formats.

Plug-ins again

The formats I've described here can be saved in many image-editing programs, but there are others appearing on the market that you can introduce as plug-ins. One of the best is a superb compression format called Genuine Fractals. This not only reduces the file size dramatically, but also allows the image to be enlarged way beyond its intended size. It encodes the image and uses wavelet technology to open and rescale with little loss in quality.

You have a number of options when saving using Genuine Fractals. The best is lossless which reduces the file to half its original size or near lossless that allows 5× compression. Both save the file as .stn format.

You can also save pictures as .fif files which allows 10× compression, and even then image quality is good when enlarged to at least its original size.

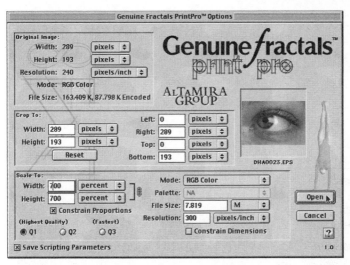

When opening an image that has been saved as a .fif or .stn Genuine Fractals format, you have a choice of the size and colour mode that you open it up to.

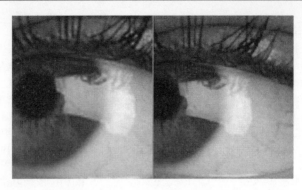

Left: A JPEG image that's been increased in size by interpolation in Photoshop. Right: The same original increased using Genuine Fractals. tice how much sharper the edges are. (See colour plate 15.)

When you're working with images of all types, it makes sense to add a program like Hijaak to your system. This can read and convert just about anything you throw at it.

13 | PRINTING YOUR PICTURES

Once you've been bitten by the digital bug and have become familiar with the software to create stunning images you'll be eager to show them to friends, colleagues and family. You may want to pin them up on the wall or even send them off to a magazine in the hope of having them published. Now it's time to look at how to get the image that's appearing on the computer screen onto paper.

While many photo-processing shops now offer services to make prints from your digital files, the most convenient way is to attach a printer to the computer. If you already have a printer and it's more than a few years old the chances are you will have been disappointed by the quality when trying to print photographs. A few years ago photo quality printers cost thousands of pounds, but the cost has come down so much that one capable of photo quality is now easily affordable.

What type of printer?

There are several types of printer to choose from – the main four are inkjet, dye-sublimation, laser and pictography.

Inkjet printers are the types that have taken the home-imaging market by storm. Companies such as Epson, Lexmark and Hewlett-Packard are producing stunning quality and delivering them to shops at low, low prices. The market's competitive and, as a result, photo quality costs as little as £90, making them perfect for home use. The latest photo quality printers from Epson include light cyan and light magenta inks along with the standard three-colour cartridges to improve continuous tones and make very realistic prints.

Epson's A3 inkjet printer is about as versatile as they come.

Sony's Digital printer works with Memory Stick and uses dye-sublimiation technology for long-lasting prints.

Dye-sublimation tends to give a more natural result with no visible dots, but these are still very expensive, costing around £600 for an A6 enprint sized model. Some digital camera manufacturers are now selling this type of printer to hook straight up to the camera for computer-free digital photography.

Laser printers deliver the results much faster than the other types, but, like dye-sublimation, are costly and often don't deliver the same quality.

Pictography was developed by Fuji and delivers prints that are indistinguishable from conventional photographs. Once again, at around £6,000, this type of printer is too expensive for home use.

How they work

All printers, like digital cameras and scanners, are graded by their resolution. A printer has dots per inch to determine resolution rather than pixels per inch, but the principle is more or less the same. Basic printers offer 300 dpi resolution and the more advanced models produce 1440 dpi. The figure is the number of dots laid down across the paper, but not necessarily the requirement of the source picture. For instance, a 1440 dpi printer may lay down 1440 dots per inch but it may use six different coloured ink dots to make up one accurate colour. This is known as dithering and means that the actual file size required could be as low as 240 dpi (1440/6).

The printer has a paper feeder that slowly draws the paper through the unit and a print head travels across the carriage width spraying the dots of ink from the ink cartridge onto the paper. The skill of the printer manufacturer is to develop smaller dots, faster travelling ink heads, more accurate colours and inks that dry quickly. This is quite a challenge but it's one that's being met extremely well.

The way the ink comes out of the cartridge to the print head and onto the paper varies with each manufacturer. Canon, for example, uses a heated element to form a bubble of ink that drops onto the paper, while Epson uses Piezo crystal to vibrate a plate which forces the ink droplet onto the paper.

Most inkjet printers have three-colour cartridges – one each for cyan, magenta and yellow. It's possible to print black using a combination of the three colours, but the results can be muddy looking so many printers also include a separate black cartridge.

Dye-sublimation printers work like typewriters by using a dye ribbon the width of the paper that's split alternatively with three colours. The ribbon is attached to rollers and is pulled across a heated print head to make the dye vaporise and transfer onto the paper. The process is repeated for each of the three colours making it slower to output than inkjet.

Laser printers employ a laser to etch the image onto an electronically charged drum as it rotates. The charged surface picks up toner from each of the four cartridges which are then transferred to an accumulator drum and passed onto electrostatically charged paper. The paper then travels through heated rollers to fix the printed image in place. They're extremely fast, but expensive to buy and run.

A pictrography printer looks like a huge office photocopier, but delivers continuous tone results that are better than dye-sublimation. It uses a laser to etch the image onto photosensitive donor paper that's supplied on a roll. This is then transferred onto a roll of glossy paper. The process doesn't require toners or ink cartridges so it's cheaper to use, but the initial cost of the machine and its size restricts home use.

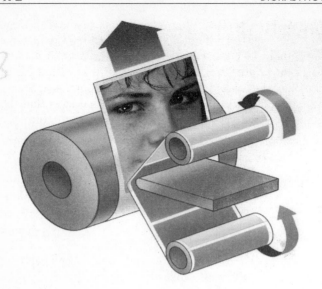

A dye-sub printer uses a ribbon with alternate areas of cyan, yellow and magenta. A heated element transfers the ink onto the paper in three passes to build up colour.

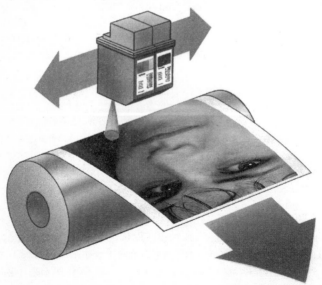

The inkjet printer's head travels across the width of the machine dropping tiny drops of ink onto the paper.

Print your digital pictures

Nearly all programs have a print option that's usually controlled by holding down the control key and pressing the p key on a PC or option and p on a Mac. When you do this the computer will access the printer that's set up. If a message appears that says that the printer cannot be found you have not set up the system correctly. First, check that the cables are all locked in place and that the printer is switched on. If both are ready open the chooser on a Mac and select the printer icon that you're using. On a PC go to the printer folder from the setting folder in the start-up menu. Right-click on the printer icon that you want to use and select 'set as default'. If the printer you intend using doesn't appear select 'add printer' and follow the on screen instructions using your printer's supplied installation disk.

You may want to adjust certain things before making a print. Going to page set-up calls up the printer's control window that lets you set things such as paper size, resolution, image size, crop marks, border and format.

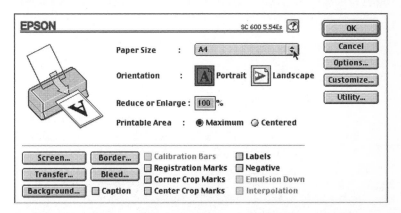

This is a typical printer interface that lets you adjust size and orientation of the paper as well as go into more advanced options to control colour and sharpness.

Always aim to set the resolution to match the paper being used and the image being printed. Also, take care when saving images to be printed. A 600 ppi image will be wasted on a printer that requires only 240 dpi. Equally, a 100 ppi image printed out on a 1440 dpi printer will make the printer look as though it's of inferior quality. Check the printer's instruction manual to find the ideal resolution to save your pictures at, but as a rough guide divide the quoted resolution by the number of coloured inks used.

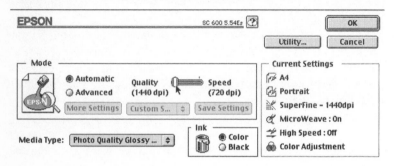

Most printers also have a paper and resolution setting to adjust and compensate for different quality papers you may use.

Don't forget to check the image size. It's a waste of A4 paper if you print off a 2 × 3 inch picture in the centre! Some image-editing software will automatically resize the image to fill the paper providing you have the option selected in the preferences. Photoshop will always output at the resolution selected so ensure it's set to the same specification as the printer in the, Adjust>Image Size box.

If you can't increase the size of a small picture to fit A4 or simply don't want big pictures try laying several out to fit one A4 sheet. Some software, such as Arcsoft's PhotoPrinter 2 or Pixology's Piccolo, allows multiple prints to be made on one sheet. Alternatively, invest in a low-cost layout program such as Serif Page Plus and arrange photos as you like. The advantage with this route is that you can also add text captions or fancy patterns and graphics in between each photograph.

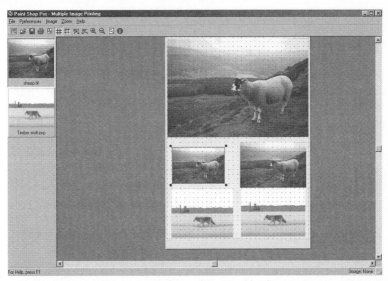

Paint Shop Pro 6 has a multiple printing mode that you can use to place different pictures onto one sheet.

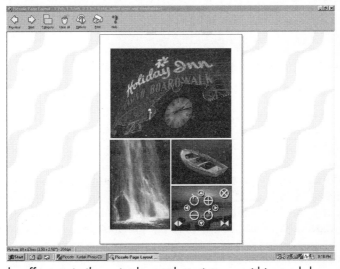

Piccolo offers a similar print layout but pictures within each box can be edited to increase the size and position of the designated frame.

Printer calibration

Okay, so you've set up the printer and the picture on screen looks perfect. So you set the printer going and wait for the picture to appear. When it does you may be disappointed. If so, you're experiencing the common problem of the monitor not being calibrated to match the printer. The image you see on a monitor is viewed using projected light, while the print is viewed using reflected light which makes it duller. These differences are indicated as the device's colour space that is defined by its gamut. You may also have been using a monitor with a colour cast and as our eyes are forgiving all your adjustments may have been wasted. Before you begin to print it's worth spending time calibrating your system. The best approach is to include your scanner, monitor and printer in the calibrations so that each ensures similar colour values throughout the process.

One way is to set up a colour management system where each item in your set-up has a colour description, known as a profile. Software such as Monaco's Ezcolor creates profiles for input and output devices and these profiles inform your image-editing software to adjust the colours to ensure accuracy throughout the process.

ICC (International Colour Consortium) profiles, are the most commonly used profiles throughout the digital-imaging world.

Another way to ensure the colours that come out of the printer are what you're expecting is to make a test strip and print that. A test strip is an image divided into segments (squares or strips), each with a slightly different colour setting. When printed you can look at each segment and see which represents the colours you're after. Then make these adjustments to the entire image and print again. Once again you can buy software to make this task easy. Vivid Details produces a Photoshop plug-in called Test Strip that automatically divides and adjusts colours for each segment. This not only helps obtain correct colour, but also density, contrast and saturation.

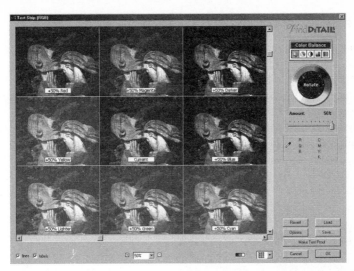

Vivid Details Test interface shows various versions of the image so you can decide, at a glance, what colour adjustments to make.

Printing paper

A calibrated system doesn't guarantee colour consistency. As in traditional photography, the paper used in your printer can also affect the colour output. Much of the inconsistency here is down to using different brands of paper, but the printer's ink cartridge can also have an effect, especially when used on a different brand of paper. You can't do anything about changing ink types as the printer has its dedicated cartridge, but you can trial several papers and find the most suitable.

Look for a paper that dries quickly and gives a bright result. Also make sure it's not too flimsy – ones you can see through tend to give poor results.

With at least 20 brands of paper to choose from, and dozens of types in each range, there's an option for most applications. The most obvious is a straight print and these tend to come in two surfaces. Glossy is the most popular as it gives a bright reflective surface and offers loads of detail. Matt, silk or satin tend to be used less as the image can look a little flat, but the advantage is you don't see reflections from the surface so it's better for viewing in bright light.

Some users prefer to have an older feel and there is a range of canvas and canvas-effect papers. These look really effective when used with portraits and some landscapes. The textured effect tends to reduce image detail, however, so you may have to print out a picture to make sure it works well. Once again make a test strip and print out sections of several photos you're considering using on this type of paper to save money.

Make your own test strip by selecting an area using the rectangle marquee and making colour, sharpness or brightness and contrast changes in each one. Write down what you did so the best can be repeated on the whole image.

To make a test strip either use a desktop publishing (DTP) program or your image-editing program. A DTP program allows several picture boxes to be arranged on an A4 page. If you use an image-editing program you'll have to create a new canvas first and then open and cut and paste parts of each image onto the new canvas, moving them into position as you go along.

Some photographers prefer to buy paper that's not actually designed for inkjet printers. Normal watercolour papers, available from art shops, can be used, providing the stock isn't too heavy or thick to go through the printer. These tend to give a soft pastel feel to the image and are great for black & white, portraits and floral pictures.

Another type of paper is transparency material that is like clear acetate and produces a see-through result, designed to be used on overhead projectors and back projection systems.

A few companies even produce water-resistant materials with wipe clean surfaces and there are plenty of sticky-backed products for making labels for various media such as CDs and floppy disks.

Kentmere and Rey & Co produce a silver-based paper that can be used for certain images to give a metallic look. Once again, this type of paper will either make or break the picture you choose so test several pictures out on one sheet.

Several manufacturers now also produce double-sided papers that can be used for making booklets, portfolio cards and greetings cards with pictures inside. If this is an area that appeals and you haven't yet bought a printer you should consider the Hewlett-Packard 970Cxi which has a special double-sided printing option. This saves you having to reload the paper and ensures the result is printed the right way up.

Special printing

Digital printing can also be used to place your pictures on other media, turning your pictures into jigsaws, cups, T-shirts, calendars, greetings cards and business cards.

Jigsaw kits come with a couple of pre-cut card sheets and iron on transfers. You choose a suitable image to print onto the transfer then iron that onto the pre-cut sheet. The image only sticks where the surface touches so when dry the piece can be separated and the puzzle's ready. Don't forget to print a second copy out as a reference image.

The T-shirt kit is similar as the printed transfer is ironed onto the T-shirt. Anglia makes a kit that also includes glow-in-the-dark paint.

Rey & Co produces a range of novel papers that includes the Party Pack and Photo Creation. The Party Pack includes cone hats, crowns, gift boxes and invitation cards that are all pre-cut to make your child's party extra special. Photo Creation is a pack of pre-cut frames, albums, calendars and postcards for fun ways to display your images.

There are also transparent window stickers that can be peeled off and reused and standard glossy stickers.

Making your own T-shirts is easy with special iron-on transfer paper.

Fade-away

One issue with inkjet printing that's causing major concern for many users is the longevity of the printed image. Over the years, manufacturers have been working to improve ink fading which affects the photograph over a period of time. It's a fact that all traditional materials will fade in time, especially when they've been stored badly, but the estimated time is around 50–70 years, whereas inkjet materials can start to show signs of fading within months and most claim a two-year life span. The problem is caused by UV light and can be improved by adding UV protection to the print.

The most common way is to mount the print behind glass that offers some protection. Some manufacturers provide a UV inkjet spray that you apply to the surface to improve the longevity. You could also consider buying a laminator and using special laminating film. In all cases, keep the images away from direct sunlight and you'll increase the lifetime.

UV spray can be used to coat the surface of the print and protect it from fading caused by UV light.

If you are a professional or semi-professional photographer who sells pictures and have now started supplying digital pictures it's important that you make your customers aware of the fading as your reputation will be at stake if the word gets round that your pictures don't last. Some photographers offer two options – inkjet prints or dye-sublimation, charging a premium for the latter. Many also stamp the back with a customer-aware message that says how to look after the inkjet print.

Although companies such as Epson and HP are working to improve longevity it's the small manufacturer, Lyson, that broke ground with its range of inks and special papers for Epson printers. They are more expensive than the standard products but claim to offer an improved longevity in the region of 25 years. Epson have also just launched a printer and ink that offers 100 years longevity.

One benefit in all of this is that even if your digital print does fade, you have the advantage of being able to reprint it with ease in the future. Just make sure you don't delete your original image!

14 | STORING DIGITAL PICTURES

Where do you keep your pictures currently? In a shoebox? Kitchen drawer? Old filing cabinet? Bin? Most of us take a quick flick through our wallets of photos when they're returned from the lab, we'll then pull out one or two out and maybe stick them in an album, or on the notice board, but the rest are destined for long-term storage. The same can happen to digital images, but there's one major advantage – it's easy and fast to log on and track down pictures. And once they're stored, you'll be able to find them with ease. That's the theory anyway!

You probably know by now that a digital picture is memory hungry – an A4 picture taking between 9 Mb and 25 Mb of space – so it won't take a shoebox worth of pictures to fill up your hard drive. So what do you do, chuck out the old pictures to make room? When a new partner asked me to throw out all my old photos that included a previous girlfriend I was devastated. These were my memories – a visual diary – and when the negative was disposed of that was the end of memories recording part of my life. If I'd had a digital version I could have safely stored the images on a back-up file and would still have them now. Similarly, what may seem like an average picture of something now may be a valuable record of history in years to come. With digital pictures that are saved on a hard drive there's the danger of losing these memories and I have just two words of advice – back up!

But what do you back up on? With the advent of digital imaging and multimedia file sizes are getting bigger and bigger. The familiar floppy disk will only hold a small number of low-resolution or highly compressed images so it's time to consider an alternative solution and there are many options.

First, let's *exclude* one – tape. While this offers the most cost-effective way of storing gigabytes of information it's not easy to access the information quickly. The reason for this is that the back up is made sequentially and the data reader cannot go to the correct data position immediately, unlike floppy disks and similar drives which are known as random access.

The system can use a DAT tape that looks very much like the cassette tape. It's usually run with a back-up program such as Dantz Retrospect. The program can work on a network, backing up several machines at once so it is often used in office environments. It runs automatically at selected times and takes a back up of the entire content of folders or hard drives and stores the info. The information is stored safely but you can't just load the tape and locate a particular image in the same way you could on the hard drive or floppy disk. The software has to search through the tape and locate the particular stream of information that can take several minutes before it can download back to the hard drive to be read.

Tape is great for back up and retrieval of your hard drive contents, but not for easy access of individual images on a regular basis.

Very few computers are now be used without a compact disk reader installed, so storing pictures on CD makes a lot of sense. Not only do you have access to over 600 Mb of space, but also the storage is safe for at least 15 years.

There are two types of CD writers: CD-R which are known as write-once media and CD-RW that are re-writable.

CD-R disks cost less than £1 each but cannot be erased so any image that you store has to be transferred back to the hard drive to be worked on and written back to a new CD. Do this a few times and you may start to lose track of which is the latest image. The best advice here is to rename the file each time adding 1 at the end, then 2, and so on.

CD-RW disks cost around £5. You still can't work on an image and replace the original, but you can erase and re-use the CD. CD-RW discs can have problems being read by many other machines, so compatibility is a big issue. They also tend to be a little more fragile, so handle with care.

Look for a machine that allows packet writing for incremental file storage.

How to burn a CD

Writing images to a CD is known as burning a CD. This is done with Adaptec Easy CD Creator on a PC and Toast on a MAC. The software locates the CD writer and checks to see if a usable CD is in place then it asks if you want to write a session or closed CD. Writing a session lets you add to and build up the contents of the CD rather than having to do it all in one go.

The software asks you to drag the folders and files you want to include on the CD into the relevant spot and then asks if you want to test the speed. Most have options to work at 1✕, 2✕ or 4✕ and the latest machines also run at 8✕. This is the speed at which the data is transferred and roughly speaking 1✕ is the duration of the CD (74 mins) 2✕ speed halves this time, 4✕ quarters it. If you say yes, the writer performs a test and confirms that you can go ahead.

Then you start to burn the CD. A progress bar will appear showing how long you have left and then a message comes up to say recording is complete and asks if you'd like to verify the session. This checks that all the data has been written correctly.

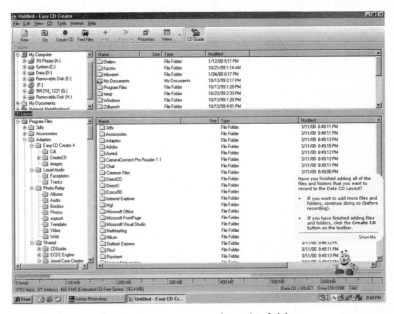

Placing data on the CD is easy – just drag the folders you want to copy into the directory and it will take care of the rest.

Other back-up systems

The most popular form of short-term storage is a removable disk drive that includes Zip, Jaz, SuperDisk, DVD-RAM and MO. When the media is loaded into the drive an icon appears on the computer's desktop and can be double clicked to open and see the contents. These offer all the benefits of the internal hard drive with the added advantage of being able to add media as you build up your database. The portable drives connect to either the SCSI or parallel interface and are available as internal or external devices. They then hold all the information on a removable disk.

Originally, Syquest led this field with large and expensive drives offering initially just 44 Mb of storage. Repro houses and printers around the world used the systems, but then Iomega appeared with Zip – a low-cost drive offering a removable disk with a more generous 100 Mb of storage space.

It didn't take long for Zip to catch the eye of consumers and so far over 14 million have been sold worldwide. The Zip disk is about twice the thickness of a floppy disk and can be accessed just as easily. It's a touch slower to transfer files to and from the computer than a direct hard drive and, although you can work on images directly from a disk, it's better to transfer the picture to the hard drive. Then do your editing and write it back to the drive, replacing the original.

On realising their success with Zip, Iomega soon launched the big brother – a Jaz drive, which holds 1 Gb of info. This was followed by a 2 Gb version, but neither has had the same success as Zip, which now also offers a 250 Mb version that will accept all existing 100 Mb disks.

Iomega have been trying to break into the digital camera storage arena, too, with the introduction of a 40 Mb drive called clik! The idea was to challenge the memory-card manufacturers with a portable drive that uses removable 40 Mb storage at a cost of less than £10 per disk. The only problem is the initial cost of the drive. There's also the added weight and bulk to consider. As memory cards are continually reducing in price and rising in capacity I personally don't think clik! will catch on.

Imation introduced a way of ensuring floppy disk users could upgrade and take advantage of newer media when they launched SuperDisk. With a drive that fits in the floppy disk drive's housing and media the same size, existing floppy disk users could upgrade and use their disks, but also take advantage of the SuperDisk with its 120 Mb of storage space. Once again it's come a little too late after Zip and struggles to compete.

The next big threat to all storage formats is DVD. It's caught on in the cinema world and will no doubt soon be outselling video cassette, but can also be used as a back-up system. DVD players are supplied as standard with most new PCs and some Macs but they can't record data. A DVD-RAM drive does and can store a massive 5.2 Gb of information. The drive also reads CD-ROM, CD-RW or CD-R and plays back audio and video CD. Unlike CD the disk is housed in a protective cassette so it's a far safer form of storage, too. The only problem at the moment is the lack of compatibility with other users, but that could easily change.

Finally, one other option is Magneto Optical (MO). The disk is about the size of a floppy disk and holds either 230 Mb or 640 Mb of information. It's currently my favourite as it has all the benefits of CD quality, with a protective casing making it safer. You can edit on disk and write over existing data, and it's claimed to have a 30-year life making it one of the longest lasting of all current digital media. MO isn't as widespread as Zip, but for home use it's perfect.

The future

If I had the skill to predict which storage system will be used in ten years from now I sure wouldn't be sitting in an office writing this book. I'd have won the lottery and be snoozing on some exotic sandy beach.

There is a big question mark over digital storage. Will it last and make our pictures as safe as the negative has for the last century? The answer still remains unknown. What if CD is replaced by DVD and then by XYZ? Will the machines of 2005 still read our disks? Imagine if you had everything backed up on Betamax videotape, or 78" records! The most positive way forward is to use the best product for now and keep an eye on where the market is going. Once you see your format fading away, back it all up onto newer technology and continue over the next hurdle.

Currently, I'd suggest CD-R for long-term storage and either Zip or MO for short-term editing.

Catalogue your pictures

If you spend time making sure file names easily identify the images they're attached to before you archive your pictures you'll find it easier to locate them later. As you don't have a lot of space to say much try using a simple code that can identify the type of picture and sub-category, for example, all pictures of landscapes could begin with LAN. Then, if it's a tree add T (LANT), in summer S, (LANTS), you may want to add the date the picture was taken (January 2000 LANTS100), you may have taken several similar images so you need to add a number at the end (LANTS1001). Get the idea? Make a note of what you're doing so you can refer back if you forget how you'd titled pictures of, say, birthday parties. It may have been PAR (party) or CEL (celebration), for example.

It's especially important to start doing this if you shoot on a digital camera, as all cameras have unusual ways of titling pictures, often with a long stream of meaningless numbers.

15 DISPLAYING YOUR PICTURES

Now you've created all these brilliant pictures how about letting the world see them? You may want to create a computerised slide show with fancy fades between each image, or you could be interested in making some money and decide to send your portfolio on disk to a potential client. It could even be as simple as wanting to add a nice border to a picture to get it noticed on the wall. Or you might be able to start a small business selling postcards or calendars of the local area. This unit shows you how to make the most of your pictures.

Create a slide show

A slide show is a great way of presenting a selection of your photos. You may have a holiday adventure to show the family or maybe a portfolio of pictures to present to a prospective client – both can benefit from a well thought-out slide show.

Several software programs will run your pictures in sequence. Some of the more advanced ones will also add a fade between each slide to make viewing more interesting. The knack is to choose the best shots and limit the show to around 20 or 30 of these. Show fewer than this and viewers may be wanting more. Show more than 30 and you'll probably bore the pants off them.

You can make the slide show more interesting by adding a soundtrack. Pick the music to suit the pictures. If it's a series of landscapes choose something classical or new age to give a tranquil and calming feel. Whereas pictures of a motorcross event will require something with more power, such as rock or electronic music.

Try to fade pictures at key parts of the music so both work together.

Look for a program that can save the show with a self-running player for other users to view. This sort of option can be saved in Mac and PC format and stored on a removable disk. The viewer can then play the show without requiring any special software loaded on their PC.

Kai's appropriately named Show has a desktop area into which you import pictures. Then, by dragging the required pictures over the sequence bar at the base, you can arrange pictures to appear in order. Next, choose the transition style and follow by adding a sound effect. There are several pre-set sounds and fades, but more can be added or customised in the Edit Room. There's also an option to add text and backgrounds.

First, bring your pictures into Show and lay them out and sort them on the desktop. Then drag the ones you want to appear in the show into the strip at the bottom. Once they're in place you can add music or text and transitions between each slide.

If you're feeling a little flush in the money department you could consider going the whole hog and buying an LCD projector to give your audience a full wall experience. The projector connects to your PC and has a lens that focuses the digital file onto a wall or screen.

An LCD projector is vital if you want to show your digital masterpiece to a large group of people.

Make your own digital photo album

A digital photo album is the best way to keep track of your pictures. You have to spend some initial time captioning the contents of your album, but once done you can track down images that are scattered all over the place, such as on your hard drives, removable disks or CDs.

The caption is used to make searching for pictures much easier. For example, if you had a picture of a boat on the River Thames at night you could include the words boat, river, Thames and night. Then you could search for pictures using the keyword river and that one would be found, along with all the other river pictures. The more details you include the better your search facility.

Many of the budget image-editing software packages have a basic photo album feature, but the tailor-made ones tend to have more features. Two commercial programs that are worth looking at are Extensis Portfolio and G&A's PhotoRecall.

Portfolio 4 is designed for the experienced user and allows unlimited database fields to be added to ensure thorough management of pictures and these can be displayed as a list, thumbnail or layout. You can also allow a catalogue to be searched from a Web browser and launch hyperlinks to Web pages directly from Portfolio. This program has a slide show mode and pages can be exported to HTML text for viewing on the Web.

It's not just for images either: graphics, presentations, movies and sounds can also be catalogued. Files to be catalogued are held as thumbnails with a link to the original so it's easy to hold thousands of items.

PhotoRecall is a more accessible package for the home user and has an amazingly simple interface. Pictures are normally stored in albums and this design looks like a digital photo album. You have a bookshelf that calls up relevant albums when you click on a subject. Then click on the book's spine to open an album. Pages appear with the pictures in place. Icons appear at the side that you click on to play a soundbite or open the relevant photo. You can turn the pages of the album or use the find file option to locate specific images. Like the slide show software a special self-running file can be created to share your album with family and friends using a Windows PC. As with Portfolio, albums can be published on the Web as HTML with ease.

Create a presentation

There may come a time in our lives when we have to make a presentation. This could be for a job interview, a budget review, staff training or selling something to a client. The convenient way is to grab a pen and a flip chart and make it up as we go along, but using a PC makes something a little special. Add pictures, fancy headings and sound to your message and the chances of getting what you want across to your audience increase dramatically.

A presentation is like a slide show in the sense that it's a series of visuals arranged in a sequence, but it goes one stage further in having advanced transitions and combines still images with moving images and text. The idea is to get over a message with impact and here is where a special multimedia program like Illuminatus will help.

Illuminatus, like Microsoft's popular PowerPoint and many other presentation programs, is available to make presenting information easy. Wizards are usually to hand to help you along, choosing the right background, placing pictures in an appropriate place and adding text. Then go beyond the basics to create stunning transitions between images or slides, have music blend in with the graphics and stunning multi-layer effects.

All stages can be played and edited until you're happy with the results. Then you can publish the package so it plays as a stand-alone presentation when sent to clients, colleagues or friends.

Take things a stage further and the presentation can be made to allow user interactivity to make viewing an even more pleasurable experience.

Produce a montage

Hippolyte Bayard (1801–1887) first considered merging pictures by adding clouds from one photograph to a second, cloudless, photograph. This combination printing led to more complex image

Digital PhotoFX designer, Chris Robinson, is regularly commissioned to create illusions for other magazines and often makes montages of clipart or digitally shot pictures. This one was for *Practical Photography* for an interview feature with travel photographer Frantz Lanting. The space at the top was deliberately left blank for a heading.

combining and the technique became known as montage. It's a clever way of combining several images into one and has been made much easier with the aid of a computer and imaging software.

Having a program that offers layers makes it easier to make seamless montages by fading the edges of each picture so they blend into each other. The technique can be used to make themed images such as the family wedding, annual holiday, birthday party, first day at school, day at the car show etc.

You could also create a montage of your local town. Go around photographing various features and then bring them together creatively. You might include landmarks such as the church, high street, statue, museum, prominent person etc. Scan the pictures into the computer, open the image editing program and drag or copy and paste each on to one canvas. Then, providing the individual images appear as objects or layers, shuffle them around and look at how each bit fits in the overall picture. Try to have images leading you into the picture rather than out so you keep the viewer's attention.

When you're happy with the image flatten the layers to reduce the size of the file.

Design a calendar

A calendar makes a useful present and is a great way of showing off your images. Many software programs provide a range of templates to make calendars. These usually have a space for the picture and print out on an A4 sheet. You could also have a go at making your own, which would really be unique, and to do this you should ideally have a DTP program such as Serif PagePlus, or QuarkXPress.

Adding frames and edge effects

Pictures can often benefit from a surround, especially if you don't intend framing them or you like to display pictures in borderless frames. There are many ways to add a surround digitally to a picture. The surround may be a border, frame or fancy edge effect.

Borders are easy to create using the pencil or sharp edged brush. Select a colour that will work with the picture content and paint around the edge.

Photoshop has a useful mode that creates a border automatically to a specified width.

Step 1 Use the eye-dropper tool to sample a colour from the picture that would be useful as the border colour. This will change the foreground colour so it's ready to be used in the Stroke command later.

Step 2 Select the entire picture, Ctrl/Option+A. The marching ants will be around the edge now.

Step 3 Go to, Edit>Stroke, Various options will appear.

Step 4 Set the stroke width in pixels. Larger numbers make thicker borders.

An area was sampled from the flower to select colour for border.

Step 5 Set the location of the border. Inside places all the border inwards from the marching ants; outside places the border on the outside of them; and centre places the border with half on either side of the ants.

Step 6 Blending mode and opacity let you choose how the border pixels react over the existing image. 100% and Normal produces a heavy colour border based on the foreground colour.

Step 7 Enlarge the canvas allowing more on the bottom to give a better balance.

Finished result with an extended canvas to set the border off against the white.

If you prefer a patterned border you first need to create a selection around the image using the lasso and + lasso. Then choose a suitable textural image and paste it into the selection. Adjust opacity and blend mode to suit.

You could also use the eraser tool to rub out bits of the edge to introduce a ragged effect or use the rubber stamp to clone from another image and create an unusual border. For instance, clone from a wall of ivy to produce an ivy border on a portrait or clone from a rose garden to produce flowers around a wedding image.

Autof/x provides pre-shaped frames and edge effects that can be placed around photographs. The pre-shaped frames are a series of photographs of traditional wooden and metal photo frames with loads more graphically designed versions. Autof/x Photo/Graphic Edges is now sold in a special four CD pack that includes 10,000 edges and texture effects. Edges can be edited when applied to a picture making the creative opportunities endless.

They are supplied on two disks with over 120 on each that can be used freely on your photographs.

Edge Effects offers hundreds of ragged edges that can be edited to vary the effects. Some give results that were only previously possible with techniques developed using Polaroid's peel-apart film.

Frame it

It's all very well adding a border and printing out the result, but that doesn't substitute the traditional photo frame. Stick a good inkjet print behind glass and hang it on the wall and I defy anyone to spot that it's a digital print produced in your spare room.

Try something a little different – look around for the panoramic 10 × 4 inch frames and stretch or crop your photos to fit. Stretched landscapes can look stunning if they're done well and the format looks interesting on the wall.

Choose your frame carefully – a heavy wooden print may make that classic landscape stand out, but a picture of the kids may require something a little more modern. Make sure the print doesn't touch the glass surface by adding a window mount and hang it on a wall that doesn't have sunlight falling directly on it as this will gradually fade the image.

Try mounting several photos in one larger frame using panelled window mount. The family tree is a good place to start. Work down from the greatgrandparents to the babies in the family. You could even put captions under each portrait and have a heading.

Share it

Share your holiday pictures before you return home. If you have a Kodak digital camera you can download free software to allow picture postcards to be created. Shoot a digital picture while on holiday. Find a shop or cyber café that gives you access to a PC, hook up to the Internet and visit the Kodak Web site: **http://www.kodak.com/US/en/digital/postcard/picturePostcard.shtml** to place your picture on a digital e-mail postcard. That will impress your friends.

Photoloft is another company that specialises in looking after your pictures on the Web. Go to: **http://www.photoloft.com** to find a great place to store pictures and plenty of templates that you can add a picture to. Pictures are uploaded to the site and appear as groups under sub-headings.

Adobe Active Share software gives you a great interface for your PC and, in collaboration with eCircles, allows images to be shared over the Internet. It's a simple way for the family to stay in touch, co-ordinate birthday parties, weddings and other events and share photos or information on the Web. Friends or colleagues who have your password can visit your gallery and take a look at your pictures.

16 MAKING MONEY FROM YOUR PICTURES

Digital imaging isn't a cheap pastime. Apart from all the hours you'll spend having fun, the cost of equipment and storage can become an expensive outlay, especially if you want to keep up to date with the latest gear. You could have a go at earning a bit of spare cash. Get your pictures out and about to show your creative talents and the rewards could be well worth the effort.

How to use e-mail and send attachments

E-mail is the fastest way to get your picture to anyone anywhere in the world.

The smaller the file size the better, as the transfer speed is reduced so the time connected on-line is reduced. The best way to save a picture for e-mail is as a JPEG compressed file. Try to make the file size no bigger than 500 Kb so that the recipient isn't waiting too long for the file to download.

Make sure you know where the file is saved and open up your e-mail program. I'm using Outlook Express.

Step 1 Click on New Mail in the toolbar, type in the address for the person you want to send the picture to and in the Subject box make it clear that a picture file is coming so the recipient knows what to expect.

Step 2 Click in the main message area and then on the Attach icon in the toolbar. Then find the JPEG file you want to send from the Directory and click on the Attach button. The Attach bar now includes the JPEG file and its size.

Step 3 The file and the message will transfer to the recipient when you click on Send. If it's big you may get a warning message.

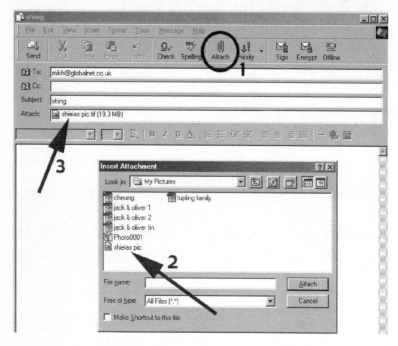

Once you've addressed the e-mail, click on attachment (**1**), select the picture you'd like to attach (**2**) and it will appear in the attachment panel (**3**).

Make postcards

What better way to show off your design/photographic skills than create a postcard. It's a low-cost item that can easily be printed out on a home printer. Pick one of your best images, crop it tightly and change the size to 104 × 148 mm. Then add a line or two of text in a colour that suits the photograph. Avoid clashing colours and ones that don't read out easily. If text can't be used because the image you have selected is too fussy, add a strip and place the text in that.

Design the back of the card so that there's room for the address on the right and either type in a message or leave space for one on the left. Make sure you use paper that prints on both sides – some have a non-ink-absorbing back so the text may smudge easily.

Look at creating postcards for towns and cities. The holiday market is more or less fully covered by the professional card manufacturers, but you may know the area better. You could supply your pictures to the card publishers or start a small business selling alternative views. Spend time looking at the cards currently available and look for new angles. Some photographers have started adding extras to pictures to make their images stand out from the usual tourist scenic views. Large moons are popular. Avoid clichés though!

I created this postcard for a local pub by taking several digital pictures and combining them on the card.

Promote your pictures

You could look at producing a postcard to sell with proceeds going to the local community or a chosen charity. Don't forget to credit the photographer and designer – that's you! And add a phone number to stand a chance of getting work from the card.

Peter Bargh photography and design

Some addresses somewhere along with a postcode
and a telephone number would be nice

Look at producing the whole package – postcards, counter display carton, price tickets etc – and contact local shops to see if they'll display and sell the cards on a commission basis.

If you start to see a demand for your work, consider using a postcard printer to produce the cards. The Postcard Company, 51 Gortin Road, Omagh BT79 7HZ, is one of the best known and offers a wide range of services with a minimum quantity of 500.

Take the postcard idea one stage further and make a card to sell your services. A larger card of around 210 × 150 mm is what most models and photographers use to pass the word around. Include one big image or several smaller ones on the front and have the details of you and what you can offer on the back. Don't include fees or rates at this stage. That's something you can discuss when the client gets in touch. Send the card to anyone who may be interested in your photography and keep your fingers crossed for the replies.

Print a CD label and make a professional-looking CD

Writing pictures to CD is a good way of ensuring the person you want to send the pictures to will be able to see them. CD is the most universal form of removable storage available and, providing you've written the CD so that it reads on both PC and Mac platforms you should have no worries. With 650 Mb of storage space there's plenty of room to supply a range of images, a multimedia presentation or a fancy looking slide show, but also room to add a CV, articles or back-up material to support the CD.

Fine. But when the CD arrives in a Memorex or TDK sleeve it won't give an impression of what's on the CD no matter how well you dress up the cover letter. What you should do is design and print a CD label, and add a colourful jewel case sleeve. Software from companies such as Neato, Labelle and SMT are specifically designed to ensure your CD looks the part. Templates are provided to allow text and images to be printed on pre-cut CD labels. You can change the layout, supply new pictures, add elements and then print out to a label. The pack comes with an applicator that ensures the label is positioned centrally on the CD and that it sticks down firmly. CDs spin at a really fast rate and become warm so avoid sticking a label down by hand; it could come away and create havoc inside the CD player.

Use a product like Neato to make impressive CD labels. It comes with an applicator to ensure the labels stick centrally and firmly to the CD.

Next the jewel case. SMT uses double sided printing paper so you can have a colourful picture sleeve outside and contents showing thumbnails or captions on the inside. Use pictures that sum up what's on the CD and be clear and concise with the caption or heading – use too many words and it's unlikely to be read.

Get pictures submitted to magazines and books

Imagine the thrill of seeing your first picture in print. Publishers and editors choose pictures very carefully, as the images need to convey what the article or book is about and they need to do this quickly and effectively. Clever pictures can miss the point and dull uninspiring ones will give off a feeling that the feature is dull and unexciting.

So how do you go about getting a picture published? Well, first, you have to send in pictures. There's no point looking and thinking, 'I could do that' if you don't do something about it!

The best approach is to study the market that you aim to break into. Check what sorts of pictures are used and how. Have a look at who's supplied the pictures. Did they write the article as well? It may be the only way to be accepted. Are pictures from libraries? Make an initial contact with the magazine or publisher and ask for the picture editor/commissioning editor. Keep the conversation brief – they're busy people. Find out first if they accept work from uncommissioned sources and, if so, what format would they accept material in. Then send a small submission of your best work that's targeted at their market. Mark the envelope for the correct person and enclose an SAE for the pictures' return.

Don't tape the envelope up so that it's virtually impossible to open and keep the packaging inside simple. The editor will want to see the contents quickly and any barriers will reduce the impact. It's a good idea to send a reference sheet with all the images showing around 2 inches wide so the editor can view without having to load and open images from the disk.

Make sure you include a stamped addressed envelope and a tearsheet of the images on the disk. Also create a cover for the CD to make a more impressive submission.

Also include a sheet of brief captions and a contact number where the editor can get more details if required.

Phoning round magazines and book publishers takes a lot of time and raises the telephone bill. You could avoid both by getting hold of *The Freelance Photographer's Market Handbook*. This invaluable reference book has lists of hundreds of markets that accept pictures. The lists includes magazines, newspapers, books, agencies, greetings card, calendar and poster companies as well as libraries. All include details of key contacts, addresses, rates of pay and much more. There's also the Bureau of Freelance Photographers, which has plenty of advice on how to approach each market. Not bad at all for £13.95. Buy this book, study which markets are suitable and make the first contacts.

Don't be put off by rejection, however. There are a lot of freelancers out there and the editors have seen many ideas time and time again. Be original in your approach and you stand a much better chance of getting your work accepted.

17 | ANOTHER DIMENSION

We have gone into great detail about ideas and techniques for digital imaging, but up until now the subject has remained on a two-dimensional format with its fairly safe 2:3 ratio, that we all know and love as the traditional photograph. The digital workstation goes way beyond this, however, and there are many more things you can do to make your images stand out from the crowd.

This unit looks at various other bits of software to take your pictures to a new dimension.

3D Effects

3D-modelling software is widely used in the film industry to make animated scenes. *Star Wars* and *Gladiator* is full of the stuff and films like *Toy Story* wouldn't exist without it. The creators have a much more difficult role to play than the 2D artists.

Many programs, such as form.Z and LightWave, come with all the necessary tools to model, render and animate.

Modelling is the first stage. Where you may start with a shape as simple as a cube, cylinder or sphere or a more complex mesh based on splines that are similar to the paths created by a Bézier pen. The splines can be rotated 360° to obtain the 3D effect.

Then you move to render and define the surface texture with its roughness, reflectivity and transparency, and add lighting and shadows. The final stage is taking the rendered scene into an animation which could be a camera moving around the object and scene or introducing movement to the model. The skill of the user is to make the model move naturally with realistic lighting so that shadows fall in the correct place as the various bits change position.

While this book is more about flat still photography we can still use 3D rendering to make pictures leap off the print. One of the most popular programs in this area is Bryce which is designed to make 3D landscapes, but can also be used to make backgrounds for subjects we cut out of everyday pictures. If you're really skilled with the program you can create near photo-quality landscapes too.

Step 1 The first stage is to open up the program and create a new terrain.

Step 2 Pick from the pre-set ranges or start from scratch and make your own terrain. Then, in the Terrain Editor, adjust the size, shape and form of the terrain.

Step 3 Choose a suitable material for the hills and adjust various properties in the Materials Lab to make it look natural.

Step 4 Adjust the angle at which it appears and the height.

A tree was added to the bleak landscape. This image could then be imported into Photoshop and other elements could be added from real photos.

Step 5 Add a sky to the background, choose the type and lighting.

Step 6 Add trees and other objects if required.

Step 7 Save the picture as a JPEG and close.

Step 8 Open up Brycescape in your image-editing program and copy and paste the subject that you want to add to the scene.

Stretch pictures using Super Goo

Super Goo is a crazy program by Kai Krause that lets you make faces from a range of pictures provided on the program's CD in the Fusion Room. You start with a bare head and add one of many pictures of eyes, hair, nose and ears. It's the digital version of Mr Potato Head!

Then you save the picture and take it into the Goo Room. Here you have the option of stretching or distorting parts of the picture to make crazy portraits. You can also play around with your own photographs by importing them into the program and adding the face parts or distortion effects.

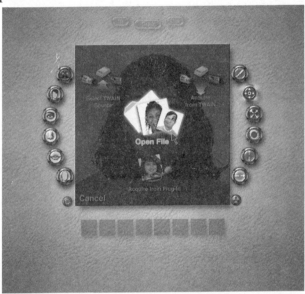

Edited pictures can be saved as Goo files or as Tiffs and JPEGS for use in other programs. And you have the option of printing out the results. Set the preference to high-res mode if you do intend to print out your results. (See colour plate 14.)

Set high-res mode if you intend printing the pictures later. Click on open file to bring a picture into Goo. The imported picture appears in the centre of the screen. There is a series of clipart male and female hair styles, noses, eyes, mouths and faces. Here, hair and glass have been added – cool or what!

Spreading yourself thin

If you've ever come across the work of Colin Prior the panoramic bug has probably already bitten you. Colin uses a special 6 × 17 cm camera to create elongated landscape pictures and has been commissioned to shoot the British Airways calendars for several years now. His work has appeared in various exhibitions and books. Check his Web site at: **http://www.earthgallery.net**. He's just one of many who have become absorbed by this alternative format.

Panoramas

Over the last decade or so Japanese manufacturers have added panoramic modes on many compacts and single-lens reflex cameras. This is usually achieved by a switch that masks off part of the negative. When printed the picture comes out at 4 × 10 inch instead of the usual 4 × 6 inch format. In a way this is not that special a feature, as you can quite easily crop the picture at a later stage and have the advantage of a normally exposed negative, too. This is easy when using the computer and there are two ways to go about changing a normal picture and making it panoramic. The obvious solution is to use the image editing software's crop tool to take off a chunk of sky and the base. The benefit of printing your own picture on the inkjet printer is that providing the length is within the printer's capability you can adjust the width to whatever you like. You don't have to stick to the usual format, unless you want to stick it on the wall using a ready-made frame.

Another technique first introduced to me by a *Digital PhotoFX* reader, Alan Bedding, is to use the transform tool and stretch the picture. While this technique is actually distorting the image it's amazing how a landscape can still look natural. The result, however, is often far more dramatic. Give it a try – you'll be impressed!

Enlarge the canvas at each side of the picture you want to stretch. use the scale option in the transform menu and pull the picture out at each side. Go too far and the result may look unnatural.

Another method of making panoramic pictures is to take several shots from the same position but rotating the camera to change viewpoint for each one. When the pictures are in the computer, join them together to make an extra long print. Many photographers have tried this in the past using normal processing and then mounting several prints side by side onto one sheet of card. The problem with this method is that exposure can vary from photo to photo so the results look inconsistent. This is most noticeable in the sky that can look deep blue on one shot and grey on the next.

If you try the same technique using a computer you can match the colours far more easily. It's also easier to make an effective join. Better still, some programs such as PhotoVista do all the hard work by having an automatic joining feature, known as stitching. MGI PhotoSuite III comes with a stitching mode as part of the program's feature list.

The only major problem you'll encounter is that once you've stitched several shots together you could end up with a picture that's longer than the printer's print format. Owning an A3 printer is a big advantage here. Or look for one that offers roll feeding. Most current Epson printers, for example, can print out on special panoramic paper that's 210 mm wide and 594 mm long.

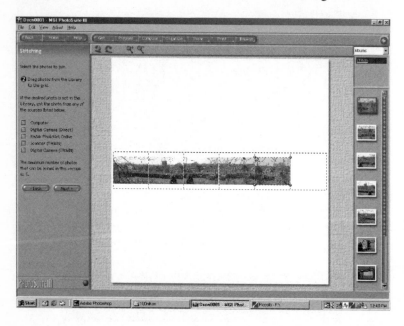

MGI PhotoSuite III allows up to five images to be joined in its stitching mode. When all the pictures are in place PhotoSuite goes to work to locate similar pixels from the edge of each picture to make an accurate join. Once joined the image can be saved and tidied up. Here, I cloned away the distracting tree branches on the left.

Tips

Here are a few pointers to make that perfect panorama.

Use a tripod to hold the camera steady.

Have a practice run without taking pictures to check the camera is level as you turn.

Use a longer lens so that more images can be taken and combined.

Allow about one-fifth of the picture to overlap from shot to shot to ensure a good join.

When the pictures are loaded onto the computer adjust colour for each image so they all match as closely as possible.

Use a graduated mask to produce a better blend if you are going to merge the pictures manually.

Add paint effects using Painter

Painter is the artist's dream software. It's even supplied in a novel 2.5 litre paint tin to make the user feel completely at home.

Painter reaches parts no other package does in providing the most advanced set of brushes and materials going. You can choose from a mass of brush styles and the materials mix and react on the digital canvas just like normal artists products would on paper.

Many Photoshop users have Painter running alongside to add paint-like effects to original photographs. There are even filter effects to turn your photos into painted effects.

One of the key strengths of Painter is its clone feature. With an image open go to File Clone to bring up a second version of the image. The original is now the source image and the new one is the destination file. Now, when you choose one of the clone brushes you can take information from the original and paint it onto the destination. The choice of effects is far superior to Photoshop. Setting Tracing Paper reduces the destination image to 50% opacity so you can draw, or trace, over the original then remove it entirely to leave a sketch of the original. This can be hand coloured or filled in using the clone brush with a paint effect. Auto Van Gogh adds his characteristic brush strokes over an image. (See colour plate 12.)

Set the Tracing Paper clone mode in Painter and the image is knocked back to 50% opacity so you can trace over the surface. Sketches are relatively easy to do in this mode, especially if you have a graphics tablet. (See colour plate 11.)

It's even possible to clone the original at a different scale and with rotation or with a level of distortion.

Painter, like Paint Shop Pro, has a set of brushes that paint repeated image patterns. In Painter it's called the Image Hose, in PSP it's Picture Tubes. This is ideal for building up a background of leaves, or a field of trees, or a street crowded with people. Just select the image or pattern and brush away. You have control over the spacing and opacity of the images as well as their direction.

Painter is also good for Web designers with its dynamic text features that let you wrap text around objects as well as stretch and bend it. There's also an image slice feature that lets you split up your image into segments so you can speed up changes by localising the change to a slice of the image. A seamless background creator lets you make up a background by repeating a small image over and over again.

Brief guide to morphing

Doctor Jekyll and Mr Hyde is one way of describing the effect of morphing. It's a technique that's used to blend one image into another with the various transition stages captured in between. It can create amazing effects, but is rarely used by photographers. You pick a suitable image and another that you'd like to turn into. Chris Kawalek decided he'd like to end up as King Tut and used Gryphon's Morph 2.5 to create his morph. The most popular morphing software is Avid's Elastic Reality.

A five-stage morph by Chris Kawalek.

Creating a morph is a fairly simple, but sometimes very tedious process. First, load two images into the morph program. The facial positions of each image should be in roughly the same area on each image. Select key points on the first image by assigning curves and points outlining the main features on each image, such as the tip of the nose, each edge of the eyes and point of the earlobes. Now move the key points on the second image to correspond to the first image. After all points are defined you basically just let the program do the rest of the work and the morph is created. To see more of Chris' work visit his Web site at: **http://www.rktekt.com/ck/**

Making moving images from stills

Paint Shop Pro comes with a useful extra called Animation Pro that lets you create animated Gifs for your Web pages. It can also be used to create flickbook-style animation using a series of continuous frame stills.

First, convert the images to Gifs. Then add them to the Movie file in the correct sequence. Now play the movie. The more images you shoot the cleaner the effect will be. This set is a series of six images taken on a Nikon Coolpix 950 digital camera, merged in Animation Pro.

Six pictures taken on a digital camera can be transformed into a fun animation with a program like Animation Pro that comes as part of Paint Shop Pro 6.

Whitographs

Having spent several years in the company of Salvador Dali, professional photographer Robert Whitaker invented a technique that involves shooting a set of close-up pictures of the same subject, each from a slightly different viewpoint. To create a Whitograph you need a macro lens with a focal length of around 200 mm to maintain a good distance from your subject and allow good control of lighting.

Decide in advance the size of the image – in this example I chose a grid of 6 × 6 images which means I needed to shoot 36 different images. Then carefully work your way around the subject shooting close-ups allowing a certain amount of overlap.

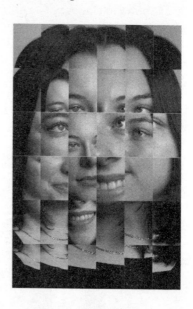

Shoot a series of pictures of a subject changing the viewpoint for each one and then save them into a folder on the computer. Using PhotoShop, open, copy and paste each picture and move them into position on the canvas. use the show grid mode to help align each layer. Alternatively, set up a grid in a design package and paste each picture into the relevant slot.

When you've completed the shoot, save the pictures and either join them using layers in Photoshop or by creating a grid of picture boxes in a DTP program such as QuarkXPress or Serif Page Plus.

This cat's about to be mosaiced! The process uses the Auto Tapestry (Mosaic) mode of MGI III. (See colour plate 15.)

18 | THE WORLD WIDE WEB

Mention of the Internet is now an everyday occurrence on television, in the national press and even down at your local supermarket. It's a powerful tool that's quickly changing the way we communicate with the outside world. In its infancy the Internet was seen by most as the next CB radio with lots of nerds using computers to talk instead of radio. Nowadays, the only way you will have escaped it is by having your head stuck in the sand. So for any emus still out there, here's an explanation.

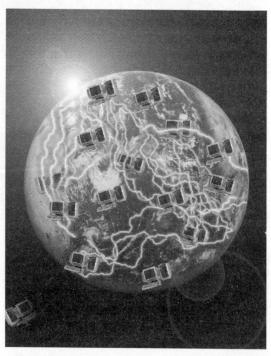

The Internet or, as it's more widely known, the World Wide Web is a huge collection of computers connected together in a network that provides a worldwide information resource that you can access using your phone line.

You can use this to log onto the Net and visit manufacturers' Web sites to check out products, visit retail centres and buy goods, speak to like-minded individuals to share knowledge, research a vast library, download software and much more.

To connect to the Web you need a modem attached to your computer and your telephone. The modem converts digital data from your computer into analogue so they can be transmitted down the telephone line as a series of squeaks and bleeps. At the other end another modem converts them back into digital data. The speed at which the modem does this is measured in kilobytes per second (Kbps) and the higher this number is the quicker data will transfer. All the latest modems are 56 Kbps.

You also need the assistance of an Internet Service Provider (ISP). They provide you with an e-mail address and a connection to the Net, referred to as a gateway. Until recently ISPs charged a monthly fee of between £10 and £20, but several companies began to offer free services and now, with over 200 free providers, there's little point in paying for the service.

The ISP supplies a disk with the software needed to get you started. The software usually includes a Web browser such as Netscape Navigator or Microsoft Internet Explorer that acts like the contents page of a magazine with interactive links to all sorts of information. It's here where you key in the address of the Web sites you want to visit. To make it easier to find unknown sites you can also install a program known as a search engine, such as Yahoo! or AltaVista, that scans the Web to locate any sites that are associated with words you type into the search window.

The CD provided by the ISP should guide you through configuring your computer so it will automatically dial your ISP when you click on the Web browser or e-mail program.

An ISP usually has its own Web site. Global.net's is like a magazine and has competitions, news and tutorials.

What makes a good ISP?

While free is usually good news it can also have its disadvantages. The ISPs job is to get you connected fast. It does this by having the right equipment including powerful computers and high user to modem ratios. Use a poor provider and you may find the system engaged when you try to connect; you'll also find it slow and it may break down regularly.

Before you sign up to an ISP have a look at *Internet* magazine. It has an automatic test facility that checks the ISP companies on a daily basis to find which are the most reliable and the results are printed in table form in each issue.

You may find you have a question and a good provider will have a 24-hour helpline that won't cost the earth and won't be engaged when you call. Some of the free ISPs charge around £1 per minute for help.

Getting good value

It's not just about connection, though. There are several other things that can give one ISP a competitive edge over another:

- Most providers will give you some free Web space so you can create a site of your own. The competitive edge here is how much. Look for a provider who offers at least 20 Mb of free space, but, basically, the more the better.

- Check to see how many e-mail addresses you can have. Five is usually enough for a family, but you may want to be greedy.

- Check that the dial-up number is local. This saves loads of money in telephone calls each time you connect, especially at peak times.

- Make sure the provider gives you access to newsgroups which are great for meeting like-minded individuals.

- Another moneysaving tip – if you are a BT customer list the ISP as your number one Family & Friends phone number and receive 20% discount.

Create your own Web page

When you've spent time browsing a number of sites you may start to feel the urge to create your own. If you did your homework when signing into your ISP you'll already have a chunk of space available to hold a site. Now is the time to fill it.

Providing you don't have big ambitions creating a Web site can be easy. A professional Web designer will babble on about HyperText Markup language (HTML) which is the code used to write a site, but we don't have to know about this when using Web design software. Software such as Microsoft's FrontPage and Adobe Pagemill hides the language in the background and includes a wizard to take you step by step through the page creation. In basic terms, designing a Web site is just a case of laying out text and pictures on the screen, choosing the size and position of each and the colour of text and backgrounds. The skill is in the position, ease of navigation from page to page, choice of images and colours – along with the speed at which the pages open and run.

As you go along you can check the style and layout by running the pages in a browser. Then, if things are going wrong it's easier to change them before you go live.

You probably noticed that the first page of a Web site is the cover/contents page. This is known as the Home page and is the page that appears if you key in the creator's Web address. It's arguably the most important page, as it has to hold your viewers' attention and entice them into the rest of the site. Make sure this page reflects the whole site and has easy navigational devices to take you further. Simple buttons that connect to other pages is all that's required. Fancy animations will slow you down.

What sort of site should I produce?

Many start a Web site by having a simple biography. 'Hey this is me, I collect stamps. Here's my collection. This is my dog. Meet my wife. This is my favourite record.' It's your chance of five minutes fame, and generally, unless you're already a well-known celebratory, five minutes is all you'll get. Personally speaking, 'Hi this is me' sites are boring. The fact that your cat is called Tibbles is really only meaningful to your family – and they know that already!

Use the space creatively to show photos that will give people inspiration. Use it to sell your products, share information and explain techniques. You could even use it to make money to fund your hobby.

If the site is inspirational and starts to get talked about, more people will visit it. (Each visit is known as a hit.) They'll start to include links on their sites to it and the more hits you have the higher the chances are that an advertiser will be interested in paying to have a banner advert on your pages.

Software needed

There are several Web design software programs available from the very basic but ample FrontPage and Pagemill to the more adventurous GoLive and Dreamweaver.

You'll also need a File Transfer Protocol (FTP) to take the pages from your desktop onto the ISP's server. An FTP, such as Terrapin or Fetch, transfers pages to the right location on the server ensuring passwords are set up to prevent anyone else getting hold of and changing data.

Let's create a Home page

We'll create a simple Home page using FrontPage Express because it comes free with Windows 98, but the process is more or less the same with other programs:

Step 1 With the program open go to, File>New>Web, to create a Web folder. Select a template from the palette that appears. You could choose one of the ready-made projects or, as I have done here, start from scratch using Empty Web.

Step 2 Choosing Empty Web calls up the title page and the cursor is already positioned with the text tool active. Simply key in the title of your page. I'm going to create a helpful site for digital image makers. I'll call it Digital Photo World.

Step 3 Now, as they say, the world's your oyster. I'll stick up a picture, Insert>Picture>From File. Once in place re-scale and adjust position to suit the other elements on the page. I've made the text heading sit halfway over the picture and changed the colour of the text on the picture so it reads clearly.

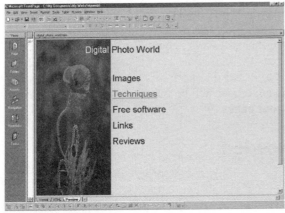

Sub-headings for various elements for the Web site.

Step 4 Add some sub-headings for various elements of the Web site. These can later be linked with the relevant pages so that the viewer can click on one to go to that area of the Website – this is known as a hyperlink.

Step 5 Create the next page, File>New>Page, or, Ctrl+N, and add pictures and text as required. You could make life simple and use one of the many templates that have been provided. Go too, Format>Theme, and click on the list to see a preview of the style of page. Choose one you like and then tailor it to your style by changing the heading font, or colour or rearranging pictures.

Step 6 To link your new page to a heading on the title page click on the heading and go to, Insert>Hyperlink, or, Ctrl+K. This brings up the contents of your Web site where you can click on the page icon that you want to link to.

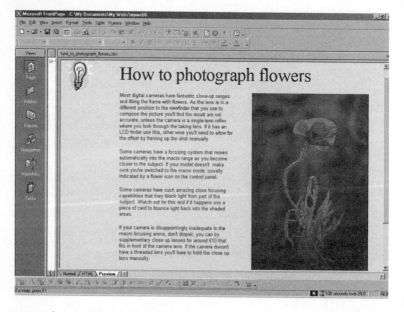

A simple page using templates provided by the Web software.

Step 7 Continue creating pages and adding links to make a professional looking site.

Step 8 Click on the HTML box at the bottom to view the script or the Preview box to see the finished work and check out that the links work.

Step 9 When you're satisfied that everything works well and you've made sure there are no spelling misteaks...whoops, mistakes, you can publish the pages to your ISP. Go to, File>Publish Web, and key in the Web address of your server. Then the pages will be uploaded to the server and ready for access when your viewers key on your Web address. Once in place, pages can be edited and updated as required.

Even a simple design like this has plenty of HTML code.

Preparing pictures for the Web

Once your site is up and running you'll soon spot badly prepared pictures when the page grinds to a halt when you try to open it. The problem will be the image size that increases the download time. When we save pictures for printing they need to be at least 170 dpi, but pictures for use on the Web only have to be the screen resolution, typically, 72 dpi. You also don't need the same depth of colour either and in many cases you can get away with 256 or even 128 levels of colour. Reducing the dpi and the colour depth can dramatically reduce the file size and increase the speed at which the image downloads and the page opens. You can judge how far to go by looking at the image on screen. If you use a program that's been designed to prepare Web graphics it will even work out which colours to drop while indicating the file size and download time. Photoshop 5.5 now comes with Image Ready that sorts all these problems out giving four versions to compare on screen.

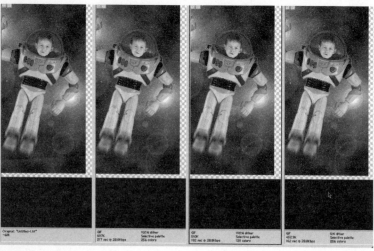

Photoshop's Image Ready has a useful comparison window to help when you need to resize and change the colour depth of a picture for use on the Web.

Finding information

All sites have a Web address. They begin with: **http://www.** but you only have to key in the bit starting with: www to go to a site. Most manufacturers' Web site addresses will be either:

http:www.companyname.com or **www.companyname.co.uk**

If that doesn't work go to a search engine and type in the name of the company. When you key the address you go to the Home page and then have to navigate around the site to find the information you require. If the site proves to be a useful resource that you'd like to visit again you can save the location in the Favourites folder which will automatically log onto the address when you click on the menu. This is known as a bookmark and saves you time keying in the address every time you want to visit.

You may not want to visit the Home page next time so add the page that's useful to your list of favourites. That could have an address like:

http:www.companyname.com/programs/moose23

– happy browsing!

GLOSSARY OF DIGITAL-IMAGING TERMS

aliasing   This is where the square shaped pixels make the curved lines of an enlarged digital image appear jagged.

anti-aliasing   Software to make jagged edges appear smoother by altering the colour and density along the edges.

binary   Numbering system using two digits – 1 or 0. In imaging terms, 0 is on or black and 1 is off or white.

bit   A binary digit is the smallest unit of information in a computer. Eight bits equal one byte.

bit depth   The more bits there are per pixel, the higher the resolution and the better the colour accuracy. Many low to mid-range digital cameras and scanners capture 24 bits of information per pixel. (8-bits = 256 colours, 24 bits = 16.7 million colours.)

bitmap   A digital image formed by a grid of pixels, each with a colour or greyscale value.

blooming   Many older CCD chips can't cope with overexposure and cause streaks or halos from light sources. It's similar to lens flare that occurs in normal photography.

bug   Defect in program that causes conflicts, erratic operation and crashes. It is usually corrected in second-generation versions.

byte Unit of computer memory; contains eight bits with any value between 0 and 255. 1,024 bytes is equal to a kilobyte (Kb), 1024 Kb is a megabyte (Mb) and 1024 Mb is a gigabyte (Gb).

CCD   (charge-coupled device) An electronic light sensor that turns an image into a digital picture.

CD-ROM   A compact disc with 650 Mb of storage space for digital images, text, multimedia and sound. CD-ROMs are read by a CD-ROM drive that's attached to or built into a computer.

CMYK   Cyan, magenta, yellow and black. Combinations of these colours produce colour images on the printed page. (*See also* RGB.)

colour depth   The amount of colour available in an image measured in bits, 24-bit depth, 36-bit depth, etc.

colour fringing   A problem in CCDs where colour filtering conflicts with information in the subject.

CompactFlash   Memory card used in cameras to store images.

Compression   A digital process that reduces the number of bits in an image so it can be stored in less space or transmitted more quickly. When an image is compressed it loses detail, which is not significant with low compression, but noticeable with high compression. 'Lossy' techniques permanently lose detail while 'lossless' methods return all the data. JPEG lossy compression is the widely accepted method for imaging.

CPU   (central processing unit) Microprocessor that determines how quickly a computer handles data. For digital imaging you need at least a 300 Mhz Pentium processor.

daisy chain   Used to describe connecting accessories, such as SCSI devices, like hard disks and scanners, or items such as keyboards, mice and graphics tablets in a chain.

data   Digital information processed by a computer.

database   A list of information, such as a mailing list or catalogue of pictures that can be quickly sorted.

DCS   Digital Camera System – name for Kodak digital cameras.

default   Manufacturers' programmed factory settings for hardware or software.

defragment   Joins together pieces of data that have been split when saved on the hard disk to make the computer perform better.

deselect   To return highlighted and selected text, graphics or checkboxes to their unselected state.

desktop   The backdrop on the computer screen where icons such as the hard disk and files appear.

dialogue box   A message box that appears on the computer screen asking for or suggesting additional information before a task is completed.

digitise   Converts sound and vision into a binary form that can be processed by the computer.

dimm   (dual in-line memory module) Plug-in memory module that increases the RAM capacity of your computer.

directory The folders that PCs keep data in.

disk A magnetic or optically etched material that data are stored on.

disk drive A storage device, such as floppy disk, hard disk, removable cartridge and optical disk drive.

dithering A printing method of making a digital image look smoother by overlaying extra colours or grey tones.

DOS (disk operating system) Operating system used by PCs.

double click Press the mouse button twice in quick succession to open a folder or launch a program.

download To transfer a file from another computer to your own, usually via modem. If you're receiving, you're downloading; if you're sending, you're uploading.

DPI (dots per inch) Indicates the resolution of a computer monitor, scanner or printer. The more dots per inch, the higher the image quality. The typical figure for a computer monitor is 72 dpi and an entry-level digital printer is 300 dpi, while photo quality printers are 600 dpi or higher.

drag Hold down the mouse button while moving the mouse to reposition a folder, lump of text or picture.

DRAM (dynamic random access memory) Common memory chip used in computers.

driver A file that controls a printer, scanner or disk drive from the computer.

drum scanner Used by professionals to produce high quality digital images. Prints or slides are mounted on a spinning circular drum.

DTP (desktop publishing) Commonly known name for producing printed material from a desktop computer.

DVD (digital versatile disk) Disk with 5.2 Gb of storage space.

dye-sublimation A digital image printing process that produces results that look like photographic prints.

dynamic range The range of light levels recorded by a CCD.

EDO ram (extended data-out) Standard memory found in PCs.

e-mail (electronic mail) Pictures, sounds and words that can be sent across a network or via a modem.

EPS (encapsulated postscript) A file format used to transfer graphic files between programs.

Ethernet Networking technology that links computers to allow fast file transfers.

expansion card   Circuit board that's fitted inside a computer to add features. Can be done with no knowledge of computers.

extended keyboard   A larger version of the standard keyboard that has a cluster of arrow keys and extra function keys.

extension   Small program that's activated when the computer is switched on and usually associated with Macs.

file format   Digital images are saved in a format that can be read by relevant software programs. Choosing the correct format in which to save an image is important to ensure it's compatible with various software. Popular ones that can be used on PC and Apple computers are Tiff, eps, JPEG, Bitmap and Photo CD.

file size   The bigger the file size the better the image. A high quality digital image could easily be around 80 Mb, which takes up a lot of storage space on the computer's hard disk. Compression software, such as Stuffit or WinZip, is available to make them smaller without quality loss.

film recorder   Records digital images onto transparency or negative film.

film scanner   Scans slides and negatives to produce higher resolution than flatbed scanners. Some flatbed scanners accept optional negative scanning hoods.

filter   Software that modifies an image by changing the values of pixels. These include sharpening and distortion filters.

Fkey   (function key) Found on extended keyboards to perform additional tasks such as short cuts to copy, paste or print.

flatbed scanner   Device used for scanning prints and flat artwork, or slides with an optional transparency adapter.

floppy disk   A 3.5 inch square, hard plastic disk with a storage capacity of 1.4 Mb that's used to store data such as text and low resolution digital images. Its name refers to the flimsy magnetically sensitive disc that's inside the plastic case.

folder   An icon that holds programs and data documents. Known as a directory or sub directory on older PCs and other computers.

font   A typeface or text style used in word processing.

frame grabber   Hardware that takes a signal from an imaging device such as a camcorder and digitises it.

gamma   The relationship between input data from an electronic image and output data telling the monitor how to display it.

gamut   The range of colours that can be shown on a computer monitor or produced in a print.

Gb   (gigabyte) A unit of computer memory (see byte).

GIF   (graphical interchange format) A popular format used to save images for use on the Internet.

gradient   A method of filling in an area with colour or a grey tone that gradually changes in density across the filled area. Also known as a graduate or graduated fill.

greyscale   A range of up to 256 grey tones from black to white.

GUI   (graphical user interface) A computer's on-screen interface, such as the Macintosh system or Microsoft Windows, that uses icons to represent computer functions.

hard disk   High-capacity magnetic disk, usually the main storage device of a computer where programs, sound and images are kept. You need at least 2 Gb if you want to do digital imaging.

HMI lighting   A specialist type of continuous and flicker-free light that's recommended for digital cameras that use a scanning exposure system.

Icon   A thumb-sized graphic used on the desktop to identify folders, files and programs.

image-editing software   Computer software that is used to acquire, store, catalogue and manipulate digital images.

image manipulation   Phrase used to describe the act of changing an image that's also known as image processing or image editing.

inkjet printer   A low-priced printer that is popular for producing digital photos. Sprays fine jets of ink onto the paper.

Internet   Usually associated with the World Wide Web, but actually the backbone of a very complex network linking computers across the globe. Used to send pictures and electronic mail (e-mail) as well as for surfing the Web.

interpolation   A software method of automatically increasing the apparent image resolution by averaging out nearby pixel densities and placing new pixels in between.

ISDN   (Integrated Services Digital Network) A telecommunications standard allowing large data files to be transmitted at 128 k per second as opposed to 56 k per second of ordinary telephone lines. It's costly to get connected and used mostly by businesses.

ISO (International Organisation of Standardisation) Used in conventional photography to indicate a film's sensitivity to light. Digital camera CCDs often have equivalent ISO ratings that can be compared with film.

JPEG (Joint Photographic Experts Group) A popular form of compression used for still images.

LCD (liquid crystal display) Either a small panel used to display modes and functions on a camera or a colour LCD screen that's used as an electronic viewfinder and to review pictures that are stored in the camera's memory.

LZW (Lempel-Ziv-Welch) a Lossless compression in Tiff files.

Mb (megabyte) A unit of computer memory (see byte).

megapixel Refers to high-resolution digital cameras with pixel resolution greater than 1000 × 1000 ppi.

memory If you intend doing a lot of image manipulation buy a computer with at least 64 Mb or RAM.

micro-dry Printing method similar to dye sublimation that fuses the ink to the paper surface for better quality.

modem Connects a computer to a phone line to access the Internet or send and receive faxes and low resolution images.

monitor The computer screen, which should be high resolution if you intend doing lots of image manipulation.

morphing Image manipulation where software is used to merge one image smoothly with another.

MPEG (Motion Picture Experts Group) A compression format used for video, animation and sound.

multimedia A file which brings interactive text, drawings, images, video and sound together.

PCMCIA card (Personal Computer Memory Card International Association) Format introduced in 1989 by a group of 25 companies to set worldwide standards for compact memory cards. They including Type I, II and III cards and are used to store images or add extra functions to a computer or digital camera.

photo CD Technology invented by Kodak that uses a CD to store and view photographs on a television or computer monitor.

PICT Standard Mac bitmap image format.

pixel (picture element) Tiny square of a digital data that contains information such as resolution, colour and tonal range to make up a digital image. The pixels meet up with each other and the greater the number the better the picture quality.

pixellation Occurs when the pixels are large enough to become visible individually.

platform The type of computer system. The main two are Apple and Windows. The latter has the majority of users and is usually referred to as a PC. Apples are in a tiny, but important minority – used mostly by design, publishing and reprographic houses.

plug-in Software that allows extra features to be added to an existing image-manipulation program.

PostScript Language used by laser printers that ensures correct placing and sizing of text and graphics, and also prepares halftones from digitised greyscale images. It's the standard way of controlling high-quality printers.

printer Image output device. Generally, inexpensive printers are inkjet or bubblejet while high-end models may be laser or thermal dye printers.

RAM (random access memory) Temporary memory that software needs in order to run its programs. Some software requires a minimum of 16 Mb to run successfully.

removable hard disk A portable hard disk with a high storage capacity with versions from 44 Mb up to 1.5 Gb. It's ideal to store or transport large digital image files.

resizing Changing the image size without modifying the resolution.

resolution Digital image quality measured by multiplying the number of vertical and horizontal pixels. A CCD with 640×480 pixels has a resolution of just over 300,000 pixels. Printer resolution is usually given as dots per inch, such as 720 dpi.

RGB (red, green, blue) Colours used by computer monitor to simulate human perception.

scanner Used to convert prints, artwork or film into a digital form. If you want to get involved in digital imaging and use existing pictures, buy a scanner.

SCSI (Small Computer Systems Interface) Industry-standard connector for computers and external peripherals such as hard disk drives, scanners and CD-ROM drives. It's mostly associated with Macs as PCs tend to have IDE to connect hard drives.

SDRam (synchronous dynamic) Memory used in PCs that's faster than EDO ram.

simm (single in-line memory module) Type of plug-in memory expansion that's being superseded by dimms.

SmartMedia Memory card used in digital cameras and mobile phones to store images.

Super CCD New type of CCD chip developed by Fujifilm. Uses honeycomb cells to increase spatial frequency and give improved quality using fewer pixels.

thumbnail Tiny low-resolution version of a digital image to help identify, catalogue or find full resolution versions.

Tiff (tagged image file format) Image file exchange format. Used by many manufacturers.

Twain (toolkit without an interesting name!) A cross-platform interface for acquiring images from scanners and frame grabbers while working in, for example, a retouching package.

unsharp mask A filter used to increase the apparent detail of an image, supplied with scanners and retouching software.

USB (universal serial bus) Latest method of connecting cameras, scanners, printers and other peripherals to the computer. These accessories can be connected and unconnected without you having to turn the computer off.

VRAM (video random access memory) A graphics card built into the computer that controls how many colours you see on the screen. The more memory the better.

wizard Software help-file that guides you through installing and using software.

WWW World Wide Web, also known as the Internet, is a mass of computers linked by phone via servers so you can gain access to vast source of information using a modem on your home PC.

WYSIWYG (what you see is what you get) Used to describe systems that accurately reproduce what you see on the computer screen on the printed output.

INDEX

TEACH YOURSELF

PHOTOGRAPHY

Lee Frost

Teach Yourself Photography is packed from cover to cover with invaluable hints and tips on all aspects of photography. Whether you are a complete beginner or an experienced enthusiast, this book provides a source of inspiration, information and ideas. *Teach Yourself Photography* tells you how to:

- Choose and use cameras, lenses, flashguns, film and filters.
- Succeed with the latest technological developments such as APS and digital photography.
- Become confident about exposure, composition and lighting.
- Process your first film and make your first prints.
- Get to grips with portrait, landscape, action, travel, still-life, architecture, nature and night photography.
- Create stunning visual effects.
- Display, store and present your pictures.

Lee Frost is a professional writer and photographer.

Other related titles

TEACH YOURSELF

QUARK XPRESS 4.0

Christopher Lumgair

Teach Yourself computer books provide a full introduction to the major software packages available today.

QuarkXPress has become *the* desktop publishing tool in all areas of design and print production. In *Teach Yourself QuarkXPress*, Christopher Lumgair introduces you to the essentials of the program, guiding you through text entry, page layout and production processes in easy-to-follow stages. By concentrating on techniques the book will enable you to create well-crafted professional looking documents with the minimum of effort.

This book:
- is an essential first guide to a remarkable DTP tool
- has clear, informative and jargon-free text
- assumes no previous knowledge of the program
- is written by a professional graphic designer and experienced trainer.

Christopher Lumgair has a BA in Graphic Design and has spent several years working in magazine and book publishing. He now has his own successful digital publishing consultancy.

PHOTOSHOP

Christopher Lumgair

Adobe Photoshop has become the tool for preparing and manipulating photographs and other still images for desktop publishing and multimedia documents. In *Teach Yourself Photoshop* Christopher Lumgair introduces you to the essentials of the program, guiding you through the scanning, image preparation and enhancement basics in easy-to-follow stages concentrating on techniques which will enable you to create well-crafted images with the minimum of effort.

This book:
- Has clear, informative and jargon-free text.
- Assumes no previous knowledge of the program.
- Combines essential techniques with guidance on the best way to scan and manipulate still images.

Christopher Lumgair has a BA in Graphic Design and has spent several years working in magazine and book publishing. He now has his own successful digital publishing consultancy.

THE INTERNET – FOURTH EDITION

Mac Bride

The Internet is the global network of computing resources forming the ever-expanding information superhighway. This book provides a clear, jargon-free introduction for anyone who wants to acquire a basic understanding of the Internet and exploit its rich potential.

Find out how to:
- explore the World Wide Web
- communicate via electronic mail
- get the latest news and information
- make new friends in chat rooms and electronic news groups
- go shopping
- do business
- play games online

Mac Bride is an Information Technology consultant and experienced author. He has written many top-selling computer books and works closely with Compuserve and other Internet Service Providers.